The Adirondacks

The Adirondacks
Nathan Farb

Introduction by Paul Jamieson

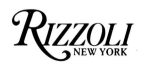

RIZZOLI
NEW YORK

First published in the United States of America in 1985 by
RIZZOLI INTERNATIONAL PUBLICATIONS, INC.
300 Park Avenue South, New York, NY 10010

Designed by Gilda Hannah
Set in Janson by Roberts & Churcher
Map of the Adirondack Park by Anne E. Lacy

Library of Congress Cataloging in Publication Data
Farb, Nathan, 1941–
    The Adirondacks.
    I. Adirondack Mountains (N.Y.)—Description and travel—
Views.   II. Jamieson, Paul.   II. Title.
F127.A2F37   1985   974.7'53   84–43072

ISBN 0–8478–0583–2
ISBN 0–8478–0584–0 (pbk.)

Printed in Hong Kong

Reprinted 1996

For Esmé and Ruth

Acknowledgments

During the two years that I worked on this book many wonderful people showed me sights and lent me their encouragement, their insights, and often their physical strength. Robin Pell, a good friend, was always a willing travel companion, carrying equipment and guiding me through the Adirondack Mountain Reserve. Krissa Johnson, an able paddler, also carried equipment and provided great companionship, guiding me through the Western Adirondacks. Vernon and Winnie Lamb of Lake Placid gave me enthusiastic help and advice at every turn. Chuck and Sue Jessie of Saranac Lake and Anne and Philippe Laumont of St. Huberts opened their homes to me at times when I did not have an Adirondack base. Philippe Laumont, who weekly took my film to New York to be developed at Laumont Color Laboratories, and his entire staff deserve special thanks for their meticulous work.

Among the many people who helped carry equipment in the field are Cindy Condon, Marshall Boris, Marty Harrison, John Edwards, Dave Flinn, Phil Gallos, Phil Hood, Shirley Rockefeller, Glen Ronemus, David Shoen, Ann Speth, Ursula Trudeau, Dan Petric, Lynne Neall, Anna Tomczak and Naj Wikoff. I met others on the trail who lent a hand for a mile or two. I will not forget them. I also wish to thank Mr. Angelo V. Ponte of Ponte and Sons, Inc., for his support and the staff of Lake Placid Center for the Arts for their friendship and encouragement.

Finally, my warmest thanks go to the people who actually helped me complete the book. First to Paul Jamieson, whose knowledge and suggestions were invaluable; second to Peggy O'Brien, who gave me her time and aided me with research; third to Anne Lacy, who with her sensitive eye and feeling for color and light helped weave important sections of the book together; and finally to Gilda Hannah and Solveig Williams for their organizational ideas.

A Note on Equipment

I use an 8-by-10-inch Deardorff camera body which is approximately fifty years old. It is fitted with five lenses, a 150 mm SW Nikor, a 210 mm Schneider-Kreuznach Symmar, a 300 mm Schneider-Kreuznach Symmar, a 450 mm Nikor-M, and a 600 mm Fuginon-C.

My preferred film is Ektachrome 64, exposed and processed normally. Occasionally I use a polarizing filter. I find that a Minolta Spotmeter-M is also an invaluable aid in measuring light.

Depending on how many lenses and how much film I carry, the equipment weighs from forty to seventy pounds.

Contents

The Adirondack Park

As a schoolboy in Des Moines I first read about New York's largest state park in a geography text. The name "Adirondack" had a magical attraction for me lacking in "Yellowstone" and "Yosemite." I did not know then that I would be living for more than a half century in a village just a dozen miles from the northwest boundary of the Adirondack Park, and that the magic in the name would be transferred to the abiding magic of the land itself.

Ebenezer Emmons, a state surveyor, first proposed "Adirondack," explaining it as the name of an Indian tribe that once hunted in the region. Legend goes further. According to it, "Adirondack" derives from an insult directed by the Iroquois of Central New York at their enemies the Algonquins of Canada. It means bark-eaters. The Algonquins were such improvident cultivators and poor hunters that they were reduced, like beavers, to eating bark.

Both the Algonquins and the Iroquois claimed the region as a hunting ground, but neither chose to settle there. For them it was Couchsachraga, the Dismal Wilderness or Habitation of Winter. As late as 1784 the interior was so little known that a geographer was obliged to admit that he could not describe it.

Some people today put a strain on the metaphor by saying that the region is still the land of bark-eaters. Sociologists regard it as a northern extension of Appalachia. Cold statistics show that Essex, a county wholly within the park, regularly has one of the highest unemployment rates in the state and one of the lowest per capita incomes. Mines are no longer worked; in most of the county soils are too thin and the growing season too short for productive farms; logging is now of marginal importance. The only big employer is the International Paper mill near Ticonderoga.

Similar economies exist in the rest of the park. Tourism is the major source of income. And certainly the tourists come, the region being within an easy day's drive of fifty-five million people. They come in the millions during July and August, with another wave during the fall color season. But the earnings of a few months hardly suffice to sustain families for the full year; the welfare rolls are high during winter. A few places such as Lake George and Lake Placid have contrived to extend the tourist season. But tourists are fickle. In 1984 Lake Placid was up, Lake George down.

The 1980 census counted 120,000 permanent residents of the park. In a land mass of six million acres this is a sparse population. The congressional district which takes in most of the park is the largest east of the Mississippi.

Some may wonder why there are any natives at all in a state park. When the park was created in 1892 there was hope in some quarters that the state would eventually acquire most or all of the land within the blue line (the park boundary as marked on state maps). But this prospect became unrealistic with rising land values. Purchases do continue, however, under successive bond issues. Recent ones and others in process of completion bring the state-owned Forest Preserve to nearly 2,400,000 acres, larger than the Yellowstone National Park and about forty percent of the total acreage of the Adirondacks. Private land consists of the holdings of year-round residents, mostly small and concentrated in villages and hamlets; of 90,000 seasonal residents, owners of lakeshore lots or, in the case of the wealthy, of large private parks; of paper companies and other owners of timberlands, which total about 1,500,000 acres. Forestry in the private timberlands is now on a sustained-yield basis, with rotational cutting of mature trees at intervals of about fifteen years. Timberlands contribute to the open-space aspect of the park.

The presence of a native population catering to visitors makes the Adirondacks preeminently a multiple-use park. There is something for every member of the touring family: storylands for the moppets; beaches for the teen-agers; museums for the grown-ups; and motels, inns, and restaurants appealing to every taste and pocketbook. Yet development of private lands is held in check by an elaborate zoning plan adopted in the early 1970s.

The pattern of multiple use also pertains in the state-owned Forest Preserve. To avoid friction among various kinds of users and lessen impact on the environment, state land too is zoned in classifications ranging from intensive use (campgrounds, ski slopes, boat launching sites) to wilderness. The latter, because there is so little of it left in the East, is of greatest significance to this and future generations. Including the St. Regis Canoe Area, there are sixteen wilderness areas, totaling over one million acres. The various classifications of state land provide for a wide range of recreational activities, from the comforts of trailer camping in well-equipped campgrounds to backpacking and river cruising in the most primitive surroundings. Camping, hunting, and fishing are permitted nearly everywhere.

Although there is overuse in some areas, the sheer size of the park and the dispersion of natural and man-made attractions serve as buffers. The Adirondack Park is the largest of all state and national parks outside Alaska. Larger than several Eastern states, it is about the size of Massachusetts and Rhode Island combined.

The eastern fringe of the park along lakes George and Champlain is the most highly developed. Wherever else the visitor enters—north, south, west—the impression of open space and forest solitude takes possession. We have a boulder, a glacial erratic, near the northwest corner of the park which for generations has had a legend attached to it. Poised between the last farm of the St. Lawrence Valley and the Adirondack foothills, it is Sunday Rock because it stands for all the constraints of civilization. Children of the valley wish that they lived on the south side of the rock where they wouldn't have to go to church on Sunday. For travelers on the state highway, passing the rock means sudden release from the box of schedules and obligations; escape into the space and liberty of the woods. There is no Sunday in the woods, nor any workday either; just the easy cycles of day and night and of the seasons.

When I came as a young man from the flatlands and cornfields of Iowa to settle in northern New York, three aspects of the nearby Adirondacks impressed me: the extravagance of uneven ground, punctuated by outcrops and erratics; the diversity of landforms; and the omnipresence of the woods, throwing a mantle of mystery over the land and inviting exploration. It was a heady experience for an Iowan.

Although sociologists associate the region with Appalachia, its rock is not part of the Appalachian chain. The uplift is an oval-shaped pendant of the vast Canadian Shield, linked by a narrow isthmus at the Thousand Islands to the Laurentian Plateau of Canada. The metamorphic and sedimentary rock of the uplift tells of complex geological change, on whose early phases we can still only speculate. The oldest rock, exposed in the High Peaks and elsewhere on the plateau, goes back one billion one hundred million years to lofty ancestral mountains thrust upward from a shallow sea which covered the eastern part of the continent. That rock has been greatly altered by later cycles of erosion, pressure, resubmergence, sedimentation, and uplift. Except on the perimeters of the region, erosion has stripped away most of the sedimentary rock, exposing the ancient, resistant Precambrian substratum.

The rock is old, says geologist Yngvar Isachsen, but the landscape is new. The diversity of landforms is due in large measure to that great plow, the Wisconsin ice sheet, the last of the glacial invasions of North America. It overrode the High Peaks of the Adirondacks and then, a mere twelve thousand years ago, stagnated in the valleys and slowly melted. The glacier stripped away organic soils, moved boulders as big as houses from one location to another, hollowed giant cirques on mountain slopes, rounded off summits and ridges, gouged U-shaped valleys, and as it melted, dumped deposits of sand, gravel, rock, silt, and clay that altered the course of rivers and impounded lakes and wetlands.

One of the facinations of bushroving over the Adirondack Plateau is reading the works of that great landscape architect. Outwash of sand, gravel, and small boulders from subterranean streams in the glacier formed eskers—long sinuous ridges which trace the course of winding meltwater streams in tunnels under the ice. Kettle holes from a few yards to a mile wide were formed by detached blocks of ice. As the blocks, covered with outwash, slowly melted, they left depressions. Some remain as dry hollows, others as bogs, and those below the water table as glacial lakes or ponds. Outwash also collected in oval-shaped mounds known as kames. Eskers, kames and kettle holes exist in great number in the central and northern Adirondacks. There are notable concentrations in the Paul Smith-St. Regis Canoe Area, near Massawepie Lake, and in the Five Ponds Wilderness Area.

The diversity of landforms is matched by the diversity of the woods. Indeed, there is a close relationship. The majestic white pine and red pine thrive in the mineral soil of glacial outwash on kames and eskers, where there is good exposure to sun. The unsorted till dumped directly by the glacier (not as outwash) is composed of a good measure of clay and silt. Till, which covers a large part of the plateau and lower mountain slopes, is suited to a mixed forest of deciduous trees and evergreens. This forest type provides the most brilliant tapestry of fall color and the most delicate pastels of spring. Where deeper layers of organic soil have accumulated during the last ten thousand years, we are likely to find a climax forest of the longer-lived northern hard-woods—sugar maple, beech, and yellow birch—with a mixture of hemlock. Tamarack and black spruce thrive on the perimeter of bogs, white cedar on stream banks and in the acidic soil of wetlands. Red spruce and balsam fir, the most prevalent of the evergreens, occupy both low swampy sites and high mountain slopes. Aspen and paper and gray birch quickly invade sites disturbed by windfall or fire. Herbs and shrubs are also diverse. A few of the highest summits support lovely alpine vegetation. Here the mean annual temperature is twenty degrees colder than in Poughkeepsie, only two hundred miles south.

The land rises abruptly on the northeast from the 95-foot elevation of Lake Champlain to over a mile at the highest peak. Forty-three "High Peaks," which range upward from 4,000 feet to Mount Marcy's 5,344, are clustered in the northeast quadrant of the park. This group offers a variety of mountaineering experience, from easy trail hiking to bushroving and technical rock climbing on vertical cliffs. Hundreds of other peaks, high enough to qualify as mountains among Easterners, are distributed over the plateau. "Elsewhere are mountains more stupendous," wrote Adirondack surveyor Verplanck Colvin in 1878, "more icy and more drear, but none look upon a grander landscape, in rich autumn time; more brightly gemmed or jeweled with innumerable lakes, or crystal pools, or wild with savage chasms, or dread passes, none show a denser or more vast appearance of primeval forest stretched over range on range to the far horizon, where the sea of mountains fades into a dim, vaporous uncertainty."

Fed by innumerable mountain brooks, fifteen hundred miles of rivers radiate outward from main axes of elevation to the St. Lawrence on the north, Lake Champlain on the east, the Hudson and the Mohawk on the south, and the Black River on the west. Some twelve hundred miles of river corridors are classified in a state river system as wild, scenic, or recreational. These rivers will remain in their natural, free-flowing state with no further impoundments and no other major alterations. Turbulent or slow and meandering, this running water carves natural museum galleries through the woods and rock in which landforms and the community of plant, animal, and bird life are on display as nowhere else.

There are twenty-five hundred lakes and ponds in the park. Several spectacular ones occupy fault zones in the High Peaks, but most are concentrated in the central and western portions of the plateau. Along with the streams that link them, they make possible canoe cruises of one hundred miles or more. In one pocketsized wilderness, the St. Regis Canoe Area, fifty-eight bodies of water attract paddlers who enjoy pond-hopping in primitive surroundings, free from the noise of powerboats.

History is of two kinds in the Adirondacks. Geography dictated a major role in world history for Lake George and Lake Champlain. Along with the Hudson River, the two elongated lakes and the short portage between them formed an easy route through an otherwise almost impenetrable forest. Whatever power controlled them was in position to control much else. The waterway became a path of empire. The Iroquois of New York and the Algonquins of Canada fought over it. Then in 1609 the first white explorer, Samuel de Champlain, with a party of Algonquins, cruised up the lake in canoes as far as the site of Ticonderoga. There with one shot of his arquebus he killed two Iroquois chieftans. This was the opening shot in a bloody series of battles for possession of the waterway. The issue to be decided was which great power, the English or the French, would dominate the North American continent. The historian Francis Parkman tells the 150-year phase of this story, what we know as the French and Indian War and what he liked to think of as the history of the American forest. The struggle for the waterway did not end with the victory of the English over the French. It continued with new contestants during the American Revolution and the War of 1812. Finally MacDonough's victory over the English fleet in the Battle of Plattsburgh pushed the English back into Canada. The beauty of the two lakes adds luster to the names of men who figured in those two-century events—Father Isaac Jogues, Sir William Johnson, Colonel Munroe, Major Rogers, Hendrick, Lord Howe, Montcalm, Ethan Allen, Benedict Arnold, General Burgoyne, Commodore MacDonough.

When Alfred Donaldson set about writing a history of the Adirondacks, he was confronted with an entirely different mass of material, fragmental and amorphous. There was no linear chain of events such as those on the eastern fringe. (At the time of Donaldson's *History*, 1921, the eastern boundary of the park was fixed several miles to the west of lakes Champlain and George.) His book is a heterogeneous collection of little histories of localities and of the disparate activities of trappers, land speculators, explorers, surveyors, early settlers, lumbermen, miners, guides and guideboat building, resort developers, visiting writers and artists, health seekers, conservationists, and legislators in Albany.

The two kinds of history are graphically contrasted in two modern museums, Ticonderoga and the Adirondack Museum at Blue Mountain Lake. At the former the memorabilia of a connected historical study is on display in the restored fort. At the Adirondack Museum a complex of buildings and outdoor exhibits represent, not a connected story, but the diverse heritage of the Adirondack interior. This museum has grown by accretion. Additions are still being made. The most recent one is a new building devoted to mining, as others have been to boats, camp furnishings, transportation, recreation, etc.

I like to think of the interior of the park as a timeless realm largely bypassed by what we usually think of as history. A land where past is present; present, future. Where a mountaineer on a high peak looks out on the same landscape today as the one viewed by Emmons 150 years ago and the same that a climber in the next century will see. Of course the timelessness is compromised by what men call progress. But much remains unspoiled as the photographs in this book bear witness.

Isolated from world and national events, the Adirondack interior has pieced together its own idiosyncratic history in many colors. But there is a thread of unity in it. History had to find an answer to the question, What is this land good for? The question was astonishingly late in being raised simply because the interior remained unknown to all except a few trappers until after the American Revolution. Then settlers from New England began to penetrate inland along the eastern fringe. By 1820 there were shallow penetrations on the north, west, and south. During the next twenty years a few pioneers settled in the central Adirondacks at Newcomb, Saranac Lake, and Long Lake.

The first systematic exploration of the interior was made by Ebenezer Emmons, a state-appointed surveyor and geologist. How little was known about the region at that time is manifest in the fact that the Catskill Mountains were believed to be higher than the Adirondacks. Whiteface Mountain was thought to be the highest peak in the Adirondacks with an elevation of about 2,600 feet. In 1836 Emmons climbed Whiteface and measured it at close to the now established elevation of 4,867 feet. At the same time he observed still higher mountains to the south. In the next year he and a party of scientists, with one artist, ascended Mount Marcy and verified that it was the highest point of land in the state. This was the first known ascent of Marcy. Mount Washington in New Hampshire had been climbed two centuries earlier in 1642.

Before Emmons' survey a few men knew what the land was good for—trappers, lumbermen already at work around the perimeters of the region, and entrepreneurs who, guided by an Indian, found a rich deposit of iron ore south of Indian Pass. But Emmons appears to be the first to articulate the question from a disinterested point of view, though his charge had been to determine the region's worth in the state economy. He found valuable timber and mineral resources and speculated on a future for agriculture. But he also found a land unrivaled for its "magic and enchantment." "I have not forgotten that my business is with geology. But while this is true, I would remember that in a community like ours, many individuals require recreation during certain seasons; and while I am occupying time and space in details of this kind, I am also making known a new field for relaxation from business—one which has peculiar advantages and many resources for restoring health and spirits, such as are unknown at the more fashionable watering places."

Few messages have ever been heeded more promptly. In August of 1837 word of the first ascent of Mount Marcy reached the outside through newspaper reports. In September the first in a long sequence of writers and artists, Charles Fenno Hoffman, came to test for himself those resources for restoring health and spirits. His report was positive, ecstatic. In his guide, John Cheney, he found the natural man, the living counterpart of Cooper's Leatherstocking hero. In the wilderness he found inspiration.

Hoffman's account of his visit to "the sources of the Hudson," which appeared that fall in the New York *Mirror* and later in book form, initiated a remarkable body of letters consisting of adventure, impressions, and ideas. "By the 1880s," remarks Roderick Nash in *Wilderness and the American Mind*, "more had been written about the Adirondacks than any other wilderness area of the United States."

This literature has given fervent answers to the question what the Adirondacks are good for, answers which influenced the legislation of 1885–1894. The region was opened in that interval of time when American intellectuals were beginning to have second thoughts about despoiling a virgin continent. Aware of America's unique inheritance of wilderness, they had misgivings about the reckless energy that was fast destroying it. A dialectic arose between exploiters and preservers. The rationale of the exploiters was tellingly put by the maverick son of a family of Adirondack railroad builders and resort developers, the late Kenneth Durant, when he described "all the Durants except me, sitting on the piazza at Saratoga Springs, dreaming of wealth in wild lands. . . . It is not so much that wilderness and Christian living are incompatible, but the parable of the talents teaches us that undeveloped land is a sin."

The lines were clearly drawn by two of the earliest Adirondack writers in the 1840s. The Reverend John Todd, in a little book entitled *Long Lake* describing the early days of that settlement, envisioned the future of the Adirondacks as a community of one million farmers and good Christians—after the trees had been cut down. Todd himself was fascinated by the wilderness; implicit in his writing is a sense of his own good luck in vacationing there *before* the trees were cut. But the idea of progress fired his imagination.

In reply, Joel T. Headley pointed out a few hard facts about climate, soil, and topography that argued against a future for farming. Then he added that he liked the trees as they were and all that went with them. "I love the freedom of the wilderness. . . . I believe that every man degenerates without frequent communion with nature." Ten years later S. H. Hammond, Albany newspaper editor, echoed the same thought and went on to propose that the Adirondacks be sealed up by the state constitution as a place where the forest grows, dies, and renews itself unmolested by man.

The artists who flocked to the Adirondacks throughout the nineteenth century were of one mind. All were wilderness lovers. They began coming with the writers as early as 1837. Charles Ingham accompanied the Emmons party in the first ascent of Mount Marcy. His painting *Indian Pass* may have been the first of many Adirondack landscapes exhibited in the cities. In the same year, 1837, Thomas Cole, the most influential painter in America at that time, father of the Hudson River School, visited Schroon Lake with a fellow artist, Asher B. Durand. Cole's *Schroon Mountain* was hailed as a "faithful delineation of wild scenery." The Adirondacks and Catskills were the favorite haunts of the Hudson River School, bent on glorifying the primitive landscapes which America had in abundance and Europe did not have.

Later in the century Winslow Homer visited Baker's Clearing intermittently over thirty-eight years. His Adirondack oils, water-colors, and drawings strike a different note. Instead of the sweeping panoramas of the Hudson River School, with its romantic vision of wilderness, Homer's art consists of realistic vignettes of life in the woods—the lone hunter with his dog, the woodcutter, the fisherman in his boat, the deer drinking from a pool while straddled across a fallen tree, the trout leaping for a fly. The moods of his watercolors are stillness, remoteness, solitude, and the mystery of these intimate, hidden details of woods life. Homer's art too was a celebration of wilderness.

The writers were not unanimous in praise of wilderness. A few preferred the European scene with its castles, villas, terraced gardens, and picturesque ruins. In 1852 George William Curtis found the aspect of Lake George monotonous and melancholy, less pleasing than Lake Como with its "imagery of ideal Italy." Writing forty years later, after Lake George's development as a popular resort, Francis

Parkman argued that the lake was no longer primitive enough: "The *nouveau riche*, who is one of the pests of this country, has now got possession of the lake and its islands. For my part, I would gladly destroy all his works and restore Lake George to its native savagery." Similar opposing tastes existed between the two brothers Henry James, the Europeanized American, and William James, who experienced "my completest union with my native land" in a moonlit night of camping under the dome of Mount Marcy. The brothers were intensely aware of their differences. After one of Henry's rare visits to the States, William wrote: "You missed it, when here, in not going to Keene Valley, where I have just been, and of which the sylvan beauty, especially by moonlight, is probably unlike aught that Europe has to show. Imperishable freshness!"

While this dialectic was going on among the writers, the woods were being ravaged. First to go was the tallest and handsomest tree of the Northeast, the white pine. The demands of the Civil War for ship masts nearly put an end to its presence on accessible sites, though it has made a fair recovery since. Next to go was the red spruce, valuable as pulpwood. Clear-cutting followed as the hardwoods became desirable for various uses. Loggers dammed the streams to float logs to mill, a practice resulting in unsightly drowned lands, with dead and dying trees and the noxious odor of decay. Some of S. R. Stoddard's photographs depicted these ravages and served to heighten public resentment.

The voices of wilderness lovers became so insistent in the 1870s and 1880s that the state legislature could no longer ignore them. Knowing that they were unlikely to get all they wanted in one piece of legislation, the preservationists joined conservationists like Gifford Pinchot in supporting the creation of a forest preserve on state-owned lands in the Adirondacks and the Catskills, to be "forever kept as wild forest lands." The utilitarian argument that finally persuaded the legislature was the need to protect the major watersheds of the state and to insure a future timber supply. The same act established a Forest Commission to administer the new law. The year 1885 is a landmark in American forestry. The new law preceded by six years the creation of national forests.

In 1892 the legislature took the further step of creating an Adirondack Park. The utilitarian purposes were reaffirmed, but with this addition: to be "forever reserved, maintained and cared for as ground open for the free use of all the people for their health and pleasure."

Meanwhile there was growing dissatisfaction with the Forest Commission. Its political appointees seemed unable or unwilling to prevent timber thefts and were even advocating the leasing of lands in the Forest Preserve. Worse, what the legislature created in 1885 it altered in 1893 by passing an act, signed by the Governor, to sell mature and standing timber of a certain size. The preservationists regarded this as a betrayal. They realized that something stronger was needed, a constitutional amendment more difficult to tamper with.

A constitutional convention was held in 1894. Otherwise a preservationist amendment would have faced a delay of at least two years and probable dilution in a rocky course through two sessions of the legislature before going to the people in a referendum. As it was, the constitution that was approved in the November elections of that same year contained this amendment: "The lands of the State, now owned or hereafter acquired, constituting the forest preserve as fixed by law, shall be forever kept as wild forest lands. They shall not be leased, sold or exchanged, or be taken by any corporation, public or private, nor shall the timber thereon be sold, removed or destroyed." (The last term, an afterthought, prohibited the destruction of trees by flooding state-owned land.) This is known as the "forever-wild" amendment. It has proved to be the Gibraltar of preservation that it was called at the time. It remains intact.

Now entering its second century, the Forest Preserve has largely recovered from the devastation of nineteenth-century logging and of the great forest fires of the turn of the century. On the private timberlands of the park logging is now selective and rotational. The streams are no longer dammed to float logs, and clear-cutting is reserved for small acreages intended for replanting.

Definitive as the forever-wild amendment seems, it has not been the end of the struggle to preserve open space and wilderness. But it has strengthened the hand of many individuals and organizations that have devoted their best efforts to this end over the last hundred years. The laws of 1885–1894 mark the first saving of the Adirondacks.

A second major threat came in the 1960s with the plans of several large-scale developers to build virtual cities of second homes on private tracts of up to 24,000 acres. Horizon Corporation, for instance, proposed to build residences for 20,000 people on a tract in the northwest quadrant of the park.

Partly in response to this threat, Governor Nelson Rockefeller appointed a Temporary Study Commission on the Future of the Adirondack Park which was to report in 1970. The adoption of its report marks the second saving of the Adirondacks. Its 181 recommendations are far more comprehensive than a simple regulation of second-home development. Now being carried into effect by the State Department of Environmental Conservation (DEC) and the Adirondack Park Agency (APA), they amount to the most ambitious plan of stewardship ever applied to so large and diverse an area. State land, as well as private, is classified and zoned. The two largest categories are "wild forest" and "wilderness." Sixteen wilderness areas (including the St. Regis Canoe Area) are designated for the highest degree of protection against the creeping tendency to domesticate the woods. They will remain, as they are now, the most primitive in the East. A hotly contested part of the plan is the zoning of private land in order to preserve open space, while at the same time safeguarding the economy of permanent residents. Many local government authorities are challenging the zoning plan as a "taking," but so far the courts have upheld it.

The struggle to save the Adirondacks is a continuing one. "The struggle that has always characterized Adirondack history," Mason Smith remarked recently, "between those who would exploit and those who would set aside and save can now be said to be, for all practical purposes, institutionalized: on the one hand, the Local Government Review Board, the local governments themselves, and the alliance of hunting and fishing associations known as the Conservation Council; in the middle, the APA and DEC; and on the other hand, the Adirondack Council, committed above all to the ideal of wilderness."

The need for a third saving has emerged with regard to the acid rain that is killing fish life in lakes and ponds at high elevations and possibly retarding forest growth. Unfortunately, this is not a simple regional problem. The solution lies elsewhere in controlling emissions from the smokestacks of the Midwest.

Except for the threat of acid rain, preservationists seem to have the upper hand—for the moment. For them the Adirondack Park, and especially its Forest Preserve, is a national treasure. Its best and highest use is as a cultural resource, an American classic, along with the *Leatherstocking Tales*, the essays of Emerson and Thoreau, the Lincoln Memorial, Winslow Homer's watercolors, and Frost's poems.

For, "when an American looks for the meaning of his past, he seeks it not in ancient ruins, but more likely in mountains and forests, by a river, or at the edge of the sea."

The legislative act creating the Forest Preserve is dated May 15, 1885. The centennial in 1985 will be one of the most celebrated anniversaries in state history. At this writing several organizations are busily making plans. None of their programs, however, can be more fitting than the pictorial celebration here offered by an individual, Nathan Farb, photographer.

The Adirondacks are a much photographed realm. Besides innumerable gallery exhibitions and the bimonthly offerings of the magazine *Adirondack Life*, three notable picture books have appeared in the last eighteen years. The present book is unusual in that Farb has penetrated the backcountry, climbed the mountains, gone on extended camping trips in order to do justice to the Forest Preserve. Comparative judgements aside, the present series of images has the power and brilliance of the best photography to arouse excitement and wonder.

Using a combination of new and old technologies and the 8-by-10-inch view camera, Farb achieves effects of great sharpness, clarity, depth, and richness of color and texture. Sharpness of detail enables him to make a focal point of some minute, exquisite object, transient with the season or the time of day, such as the reflection of a crescent moon, a luminous reddish sprig amidst snow-dusted greenery, or a single cardinal flower half submerged in a rain-swollen river.

Turning over these pages, we become aware of Farb's deep emotional response to nature. His photographs are more than factual renditions of Adirondack landscape. They are rich in the spirit of wilderness— its stillness, mystery, solitude, and grandeur.

Paul Jamieson, *Canton, N.Y.*
November, 1984

The Photographs

I grew up in the Adirondacks. The trips I made into the wilderness as a boy undoubtedly changed the direction of my life. I cannot imagine who or what I would be today without those early experiences in that magnificent, quiet landscape.

Like most young people, I suspected that the grass might be greener somewhere else. I knew that there were taller mountains in the West, in South America, Europe, and Asia, and felt that taller mountains would somehow be better mountains. Later, when I went to see the Rockies and to visit Europe, I realized that bigger does not necessarily mean better. The variety of trees, the streams and rivers, the glacial lakes and ponds, the great stone cliffs rising to form these ancient Adirondacks, and the constantly changing light and weather create a truly harmonic balance that has nothing to do with height.

The Reverend Murray, one of the first great chroniclers of the Adirondacks, reported in the 1880's that an American artist who had traveled all over Switzerland and the valleys of the Rhine and Rhone rivers wrote home from Europe to say that he had not met with scenery comparable in grandeur to that of the lakes, mountains, and forests of the Adirondack region. My experience was similar: the more widely I traveled, the more aware I became of how privileged my boyhood years had been.

About a hundred years ago, Thoreau wrote that even though Fulton had long since invented the steamboat, an Indian guide was still needed to get to the headwaters of the Hudson in the Adirondack country. Actually, while there were still some Indians working as guides, at the time Thoreau was writing, the white man had largely taken over and developed that role by the middle of the nineteenth century. These guides were men who knew intimately the woods, rivers, lakes, and mountains of the Adirondacks; or rather, each knew a part of them. The territory is far too large for one person to be knowledgeable about it all. Although often repeated by Adirondackers, it is little known or recognized elsewhere that the Adirondacks compose the largest park—state or federal—in the contiguous

Pages 26–27: Sunrise on Algonquin Peak

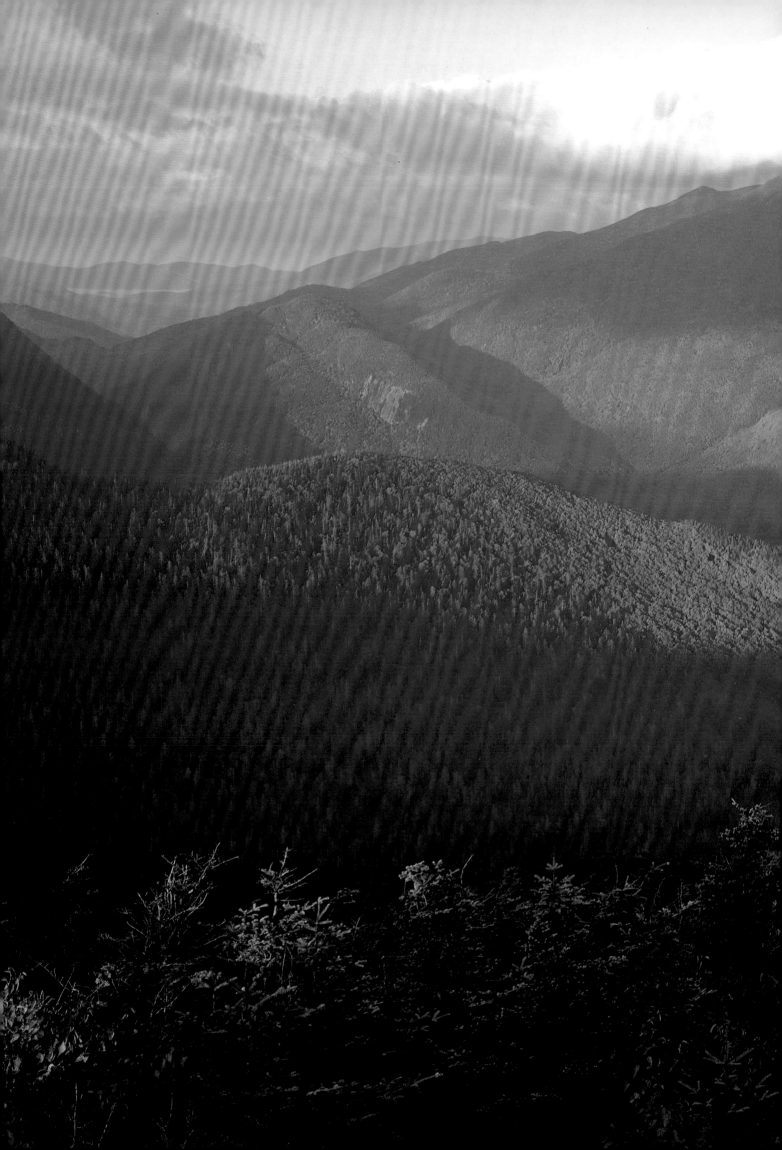

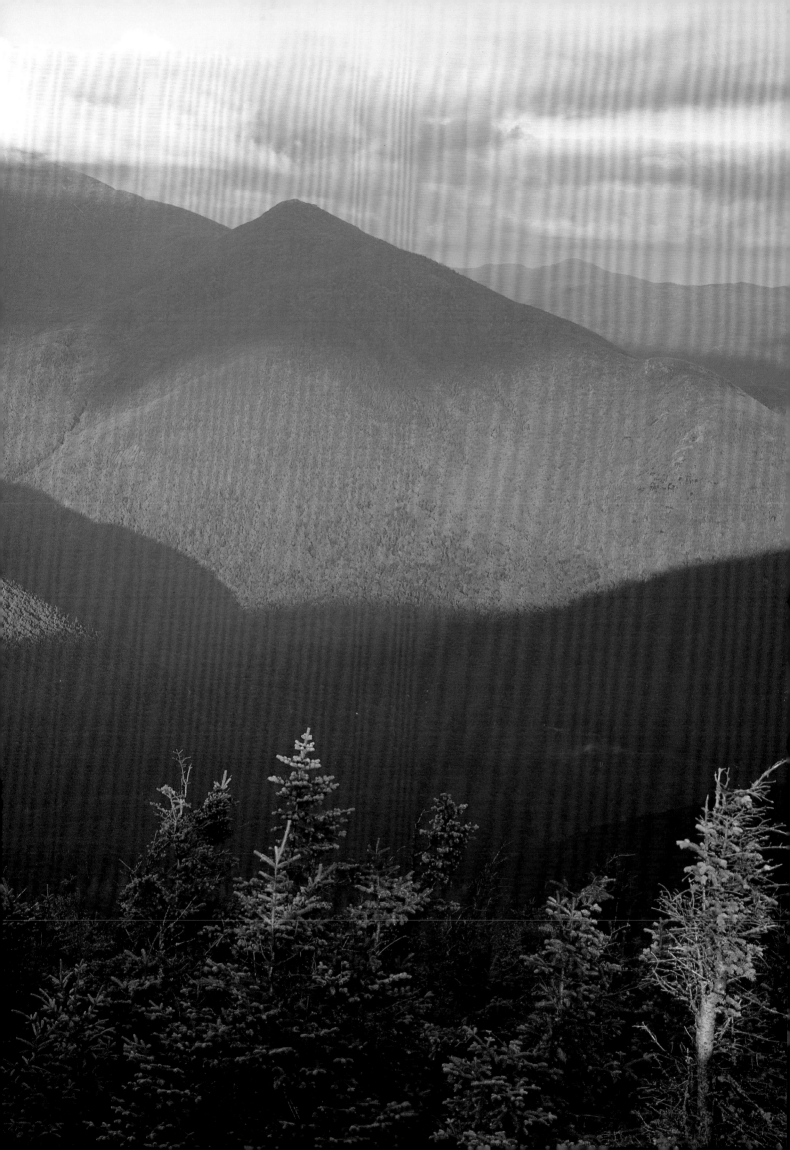

forty-eight states. It is larger than Yellowstone, Grand Canyon, Glacier and Olympic national parks combined.

The guides were remarkable, colorful characters. They hired themselves out to the wealthy, leading their charges into the woods, showing them the sights, and teaching them to hunt, fish, and enjoy the vast outdoors. Orson Schofield Phelps, who was nicknamed "Old Mountain," was a guide in the high peak region. Phil Gallos writes about Phelps in his book *By Foot in the Adirondacks:*

Phelps loved the wilderness like nothing else, like the only thing that was lasting and real in this world. To him every mountain and every brook and every lake was a special, personal friend; and the great forest was the spirit which gave life to all.

Most beloved among his wilderness friends was the beautiful High Peak of Essex, Mount Marcy, which he affectionately called "Mount Mercy." "Mercy" was more than a friend, almost a wife. It is difficult to comprehend the passion of a man who, after a long absence, casts himself onto the summit rocks and cries, "I'm with you once again."

It wasn't until the "city folk" began to visit The Valley that Phelps encountered human beings who could understand his passion, his fire, and would value it. Such men as Charles Dudley Warner, Noah Porter, Joseph Hopkins Twichell, and Horace Bushnell became his favorite companions; and they desired his presence as much as he desired theirs.

It must have been quite a scene when this child of nature sat on a log by a fire and discussed history and philosophy with a well known writer, a president of Yale, and two theologians.

The first photograph in this book was taken from the top of the mountain named after Phelps. The view, one of the finest in the Adirondacks, was not seen by European eyes until eighty years ago, and the mountain remained without a trail until the 1950's. Its first recorded ascent was made in 1904 by the American Charles Wood.

As a boy I met a few local characters who reminded me of Phelps. Their way of life and their strong relationship to the Adirondack landscape made me imagine becoming a guide myself. In a way, this fantasy has been realized. Through these photographs, I appoint myself your guide. I will take you to the places I know, just when the light and weather are perfect, and show you what I have seen. If you are one of the Adirondackers who know vastly more than I, please forgive this "trespass." In reality I am a photographer still learning about these mountains.

Streams, Rivers and Waterfalls

I lived in the town of Keene, in the Keene Valley, while working on this book. The township calls itself the "home of the high peaks." Indeed it is, but more than sensing the presence of high mountains, one is aware of being surrounded by rushing water. The Ausable River and the streams and brooks flowing into it come cascading down from the peaks to a valley floor that is about a thousand feet above sea level. Adrian Edmonds, a friend of mine, great-great grandson of William Edmonds, the first white man of record to set eyes on the stunning Cascade Lakes, took me to no less than six spectacular waterfalls in the valley. I have photographed them all with long exposures ranging from two to sixteen seconds.

At Gill Brook, which flows through the woods, there is often a sunny quality of light that is very difficult to capture because, as all photographers know, film is incapable of registering detail in the highlight areas and the shadows at once. As a result one often ends up with good texture in certain parts of the photo-graph but none in others. For this reason, I often choose to photograph in light that is diffused by haze or an overcast sky. The danger of this is that the picture may turn out dull or blue owing to the extreme sensitivity of film to blue light. On the particular day that I took the photograph on pages 32–33, the clouds were moving fast and the sun was going in and out. It occurred to me that if I could make the exposure long enough, I would be able to mix the two kinds of light. I calculated that if the sun was behind a cloud, at f45 a six-second exposure would be needed. I hoped the sun would emerge part way through the exposure. I positioned my camera by the quiet brook and prepared to use several pieces of film. To my delight, the sun came out three seconds through my first exposure. I gave it another second and had my picture. It is one that pleases me very much from a technical point of view.

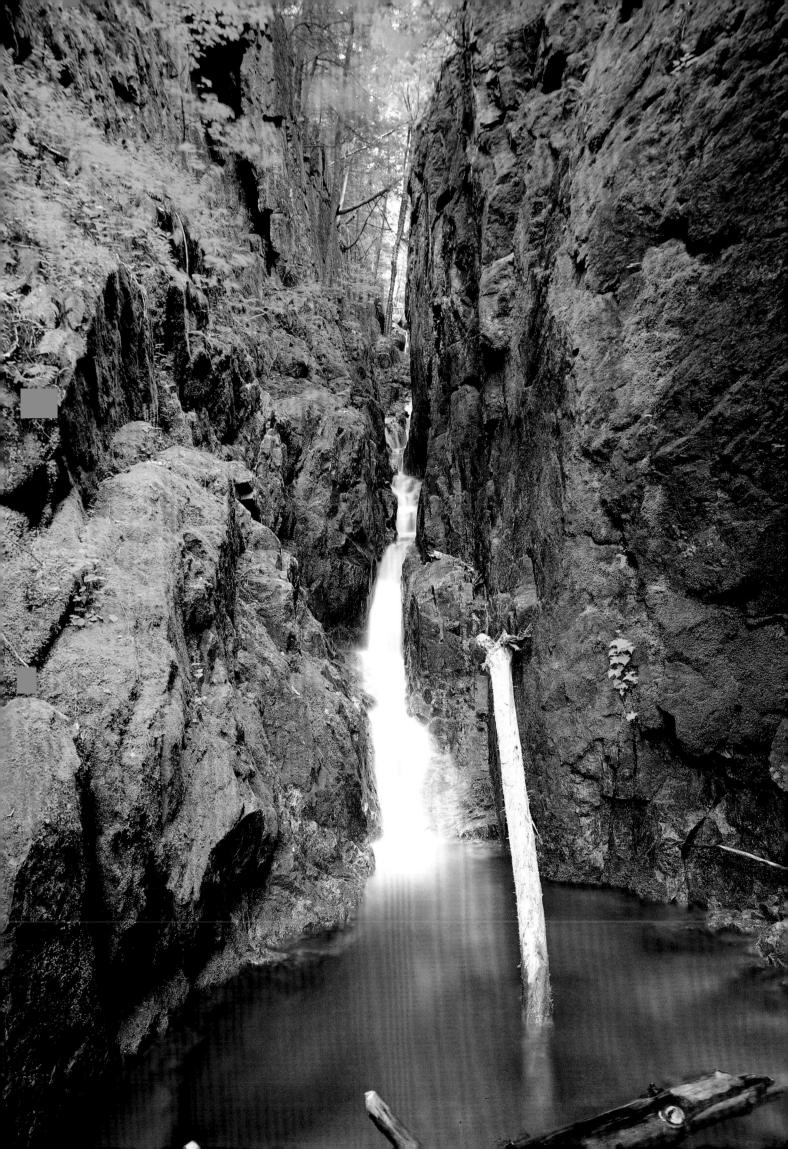

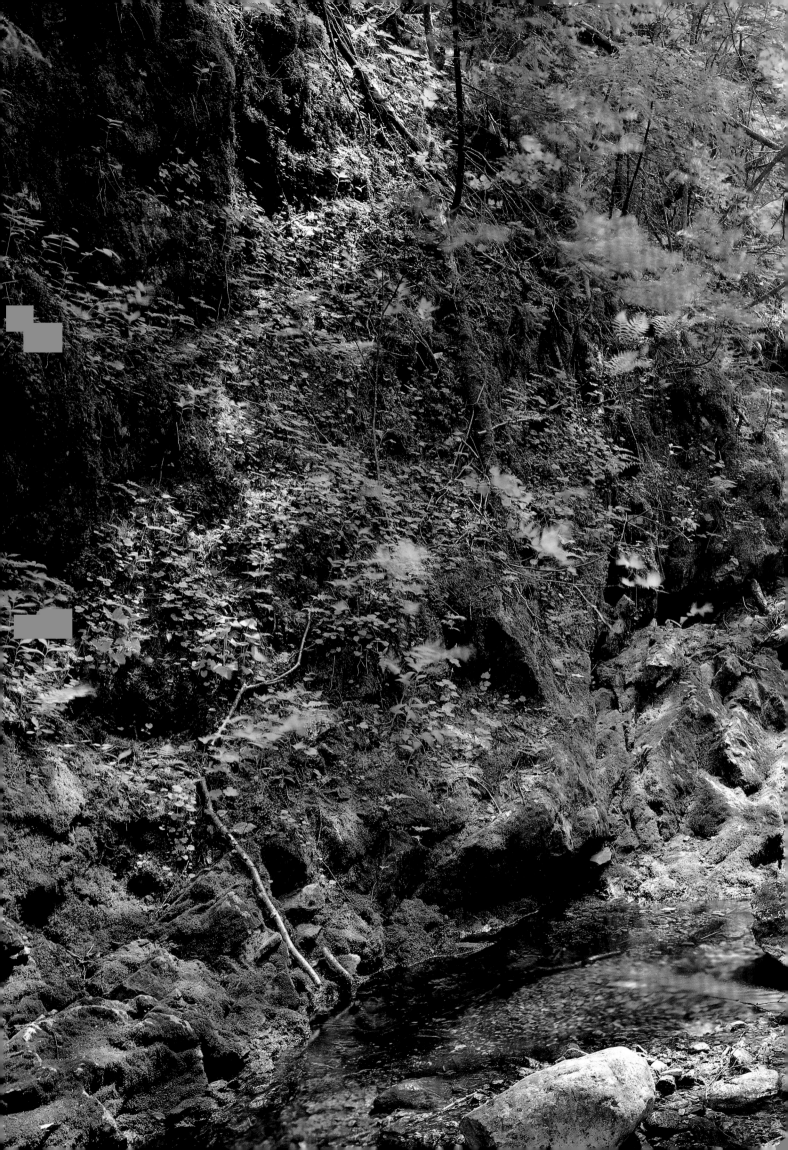

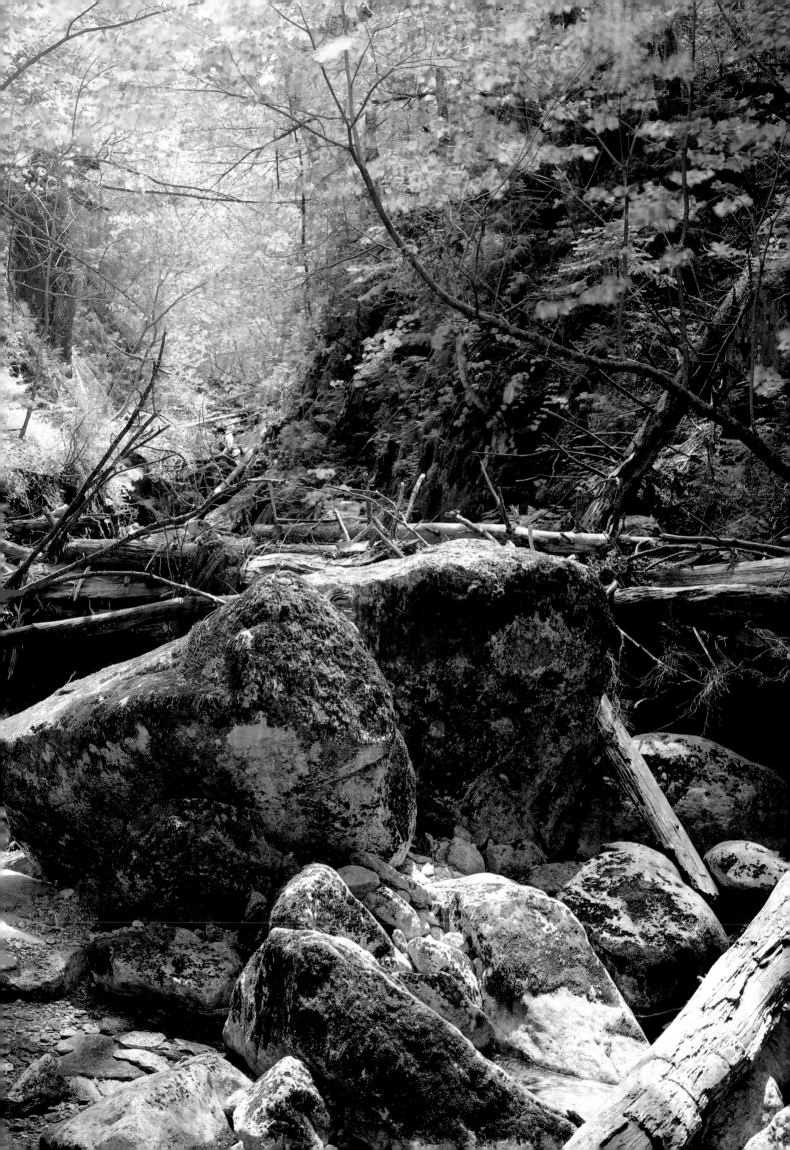

Page 35: Beaver Meadow Falls

Pages 36–37: Tannic ice at Avalanche Pass—the divide between the Hudson and Ausable rivers

Page 38: Bushnell Falls

Page 39: Mossy Cascade

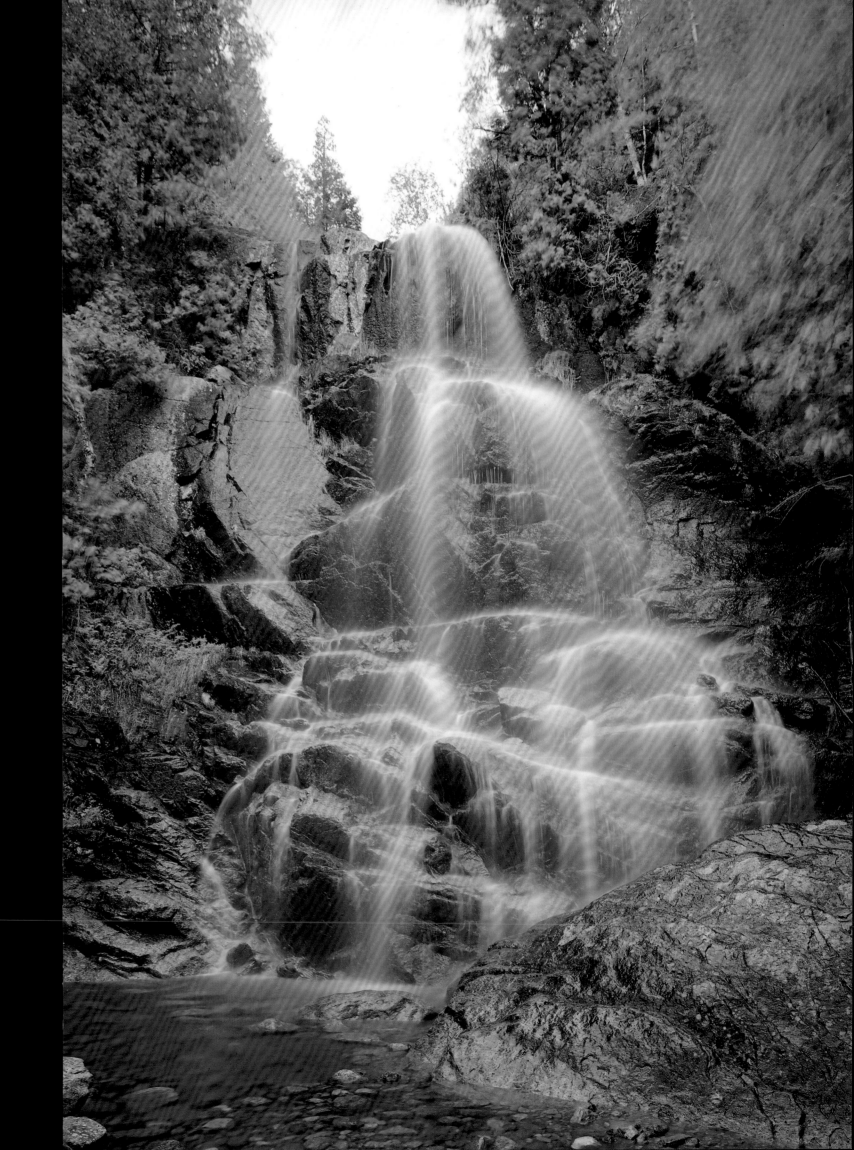

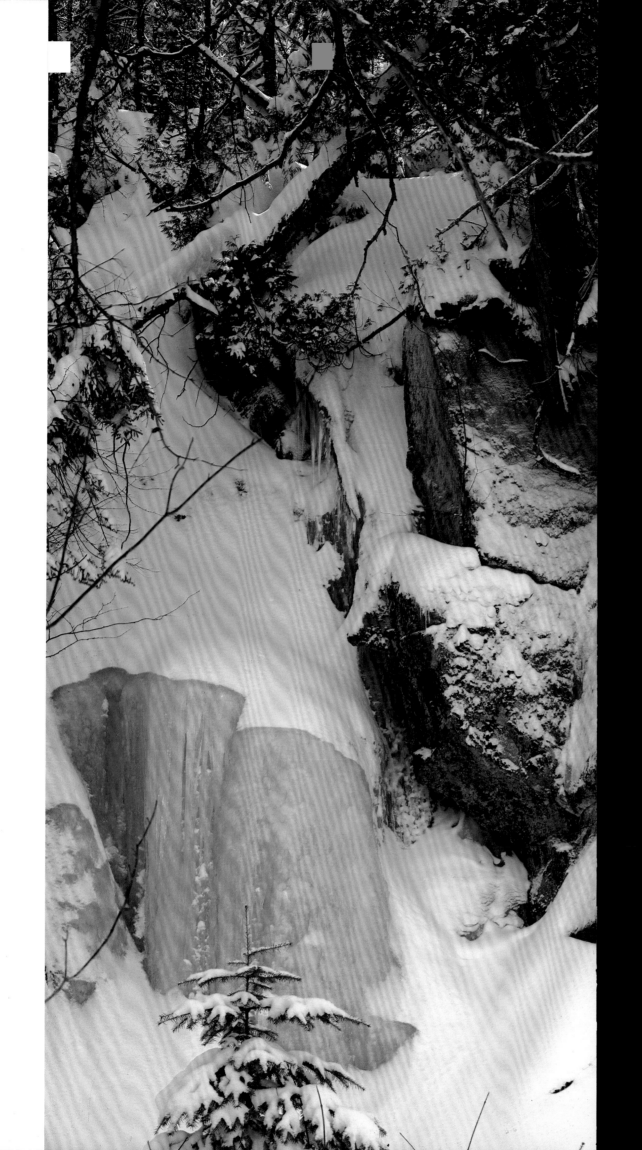

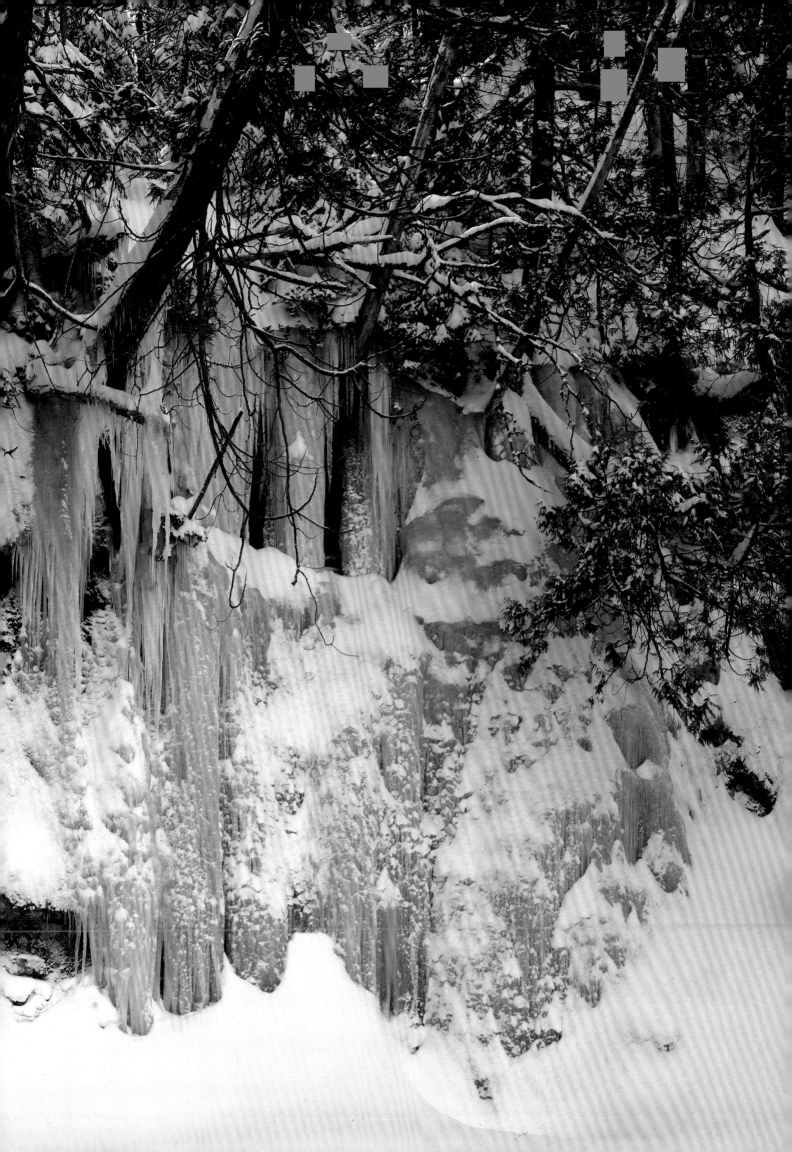

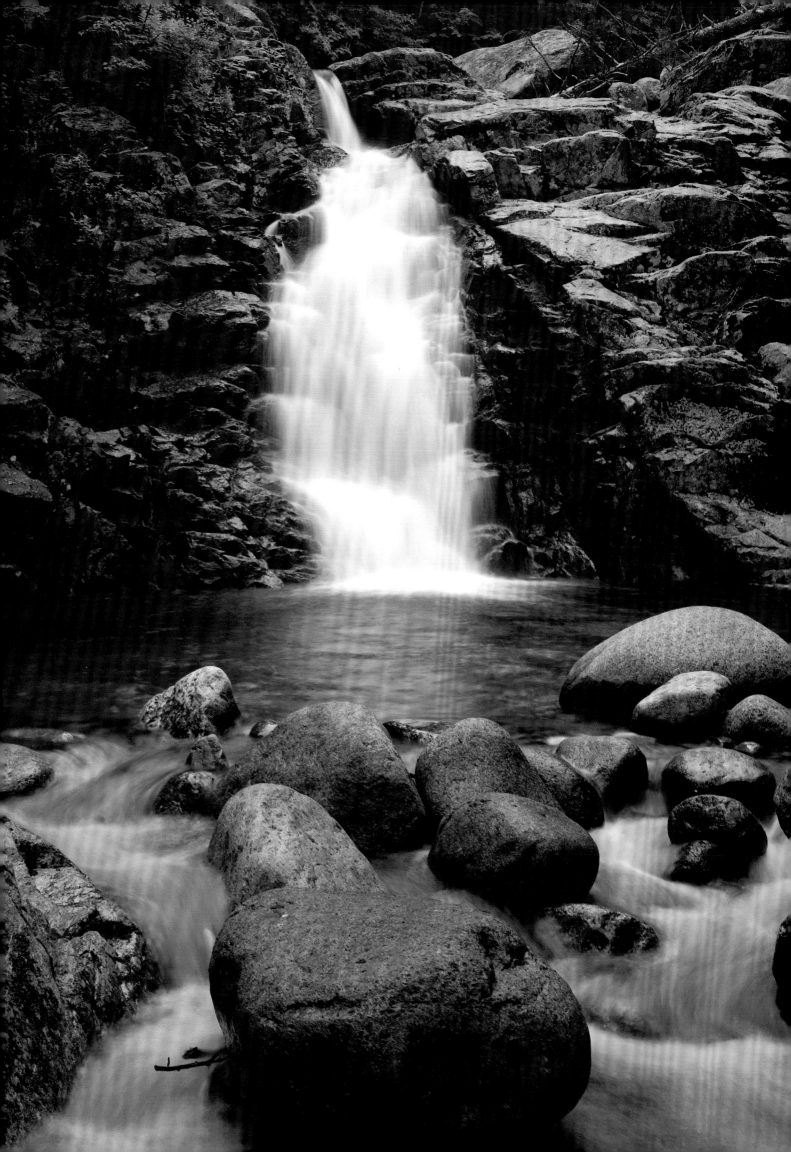

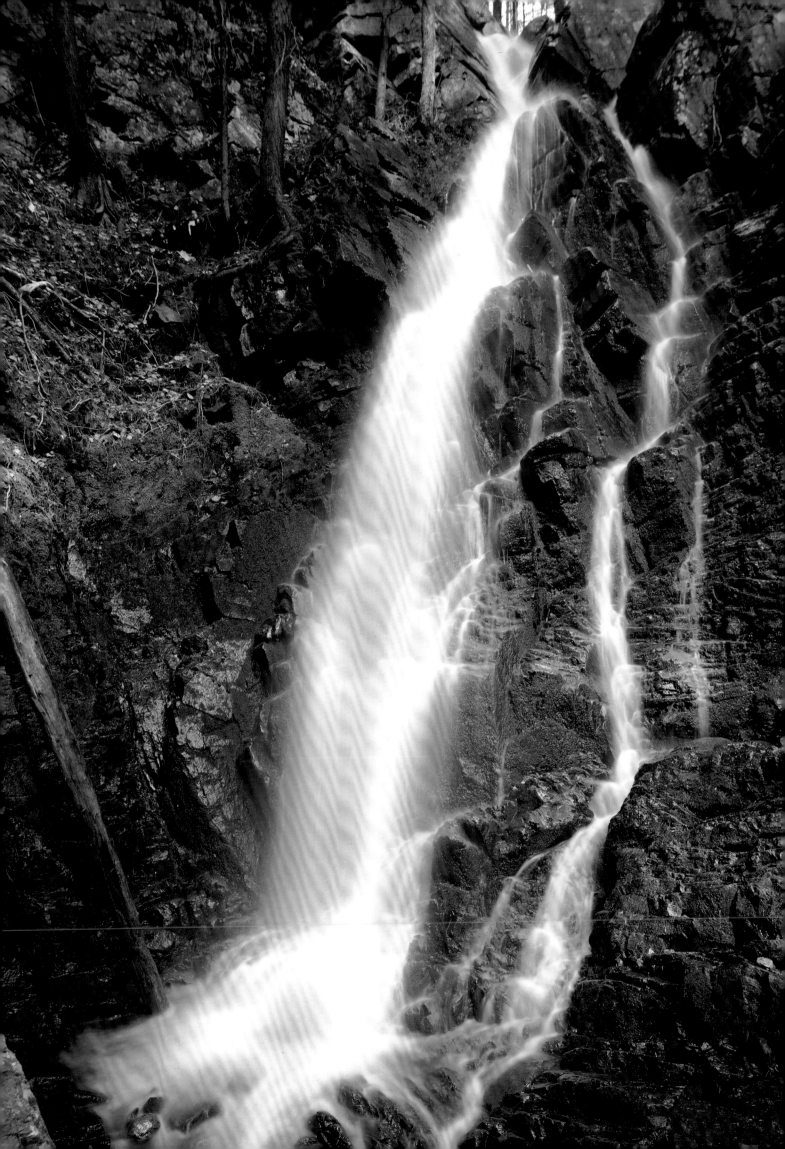

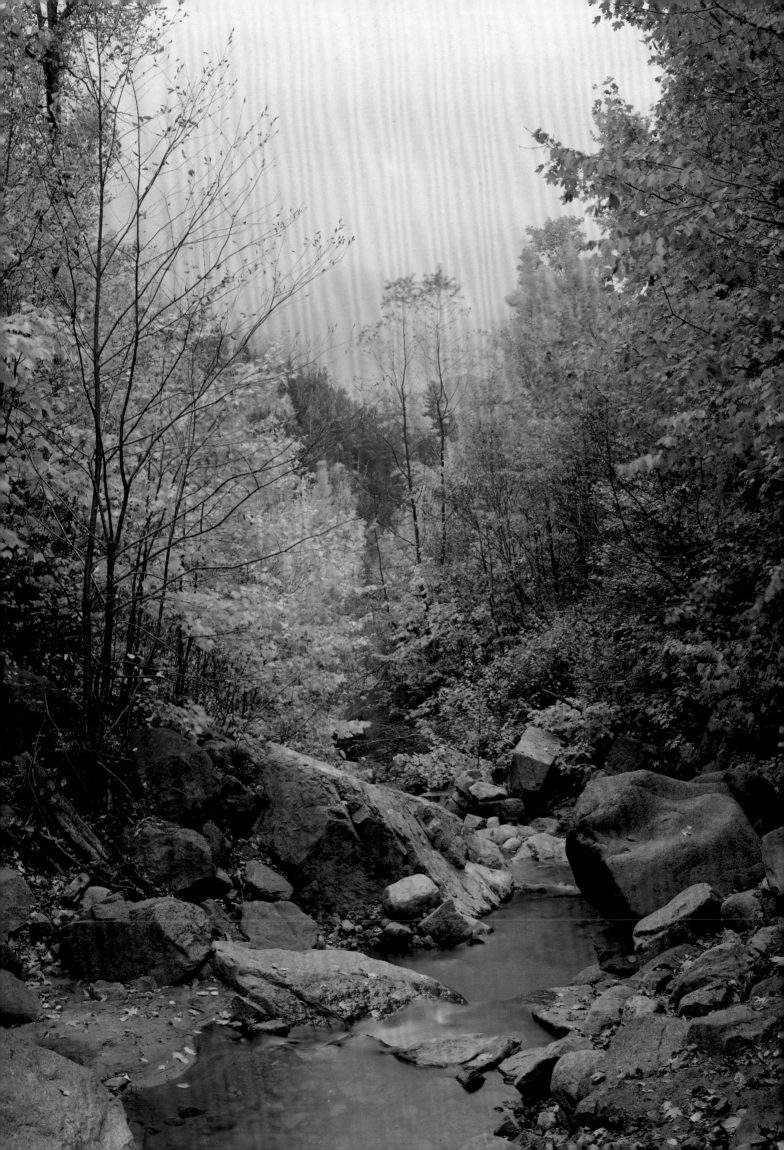

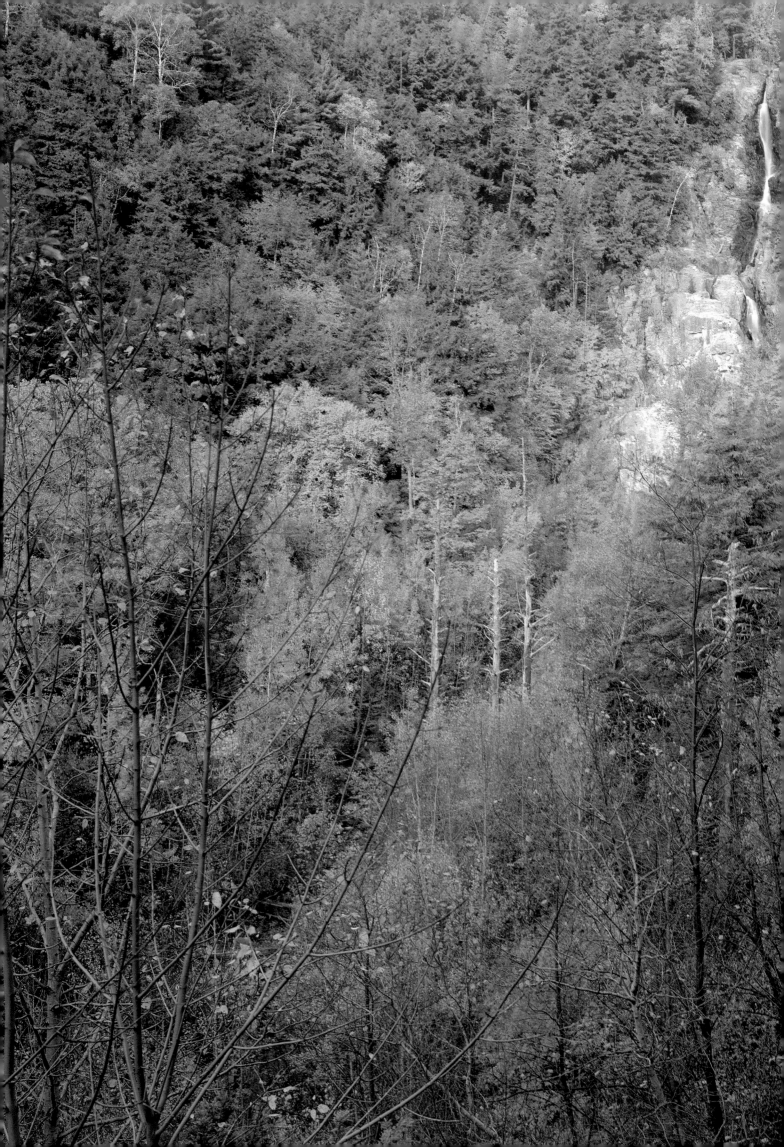

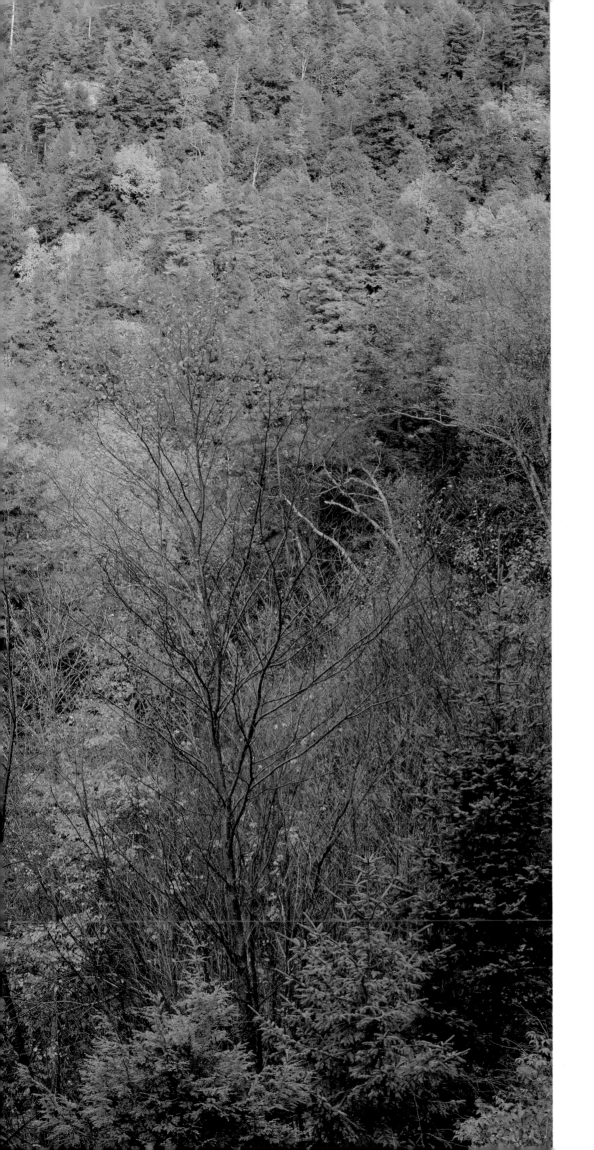

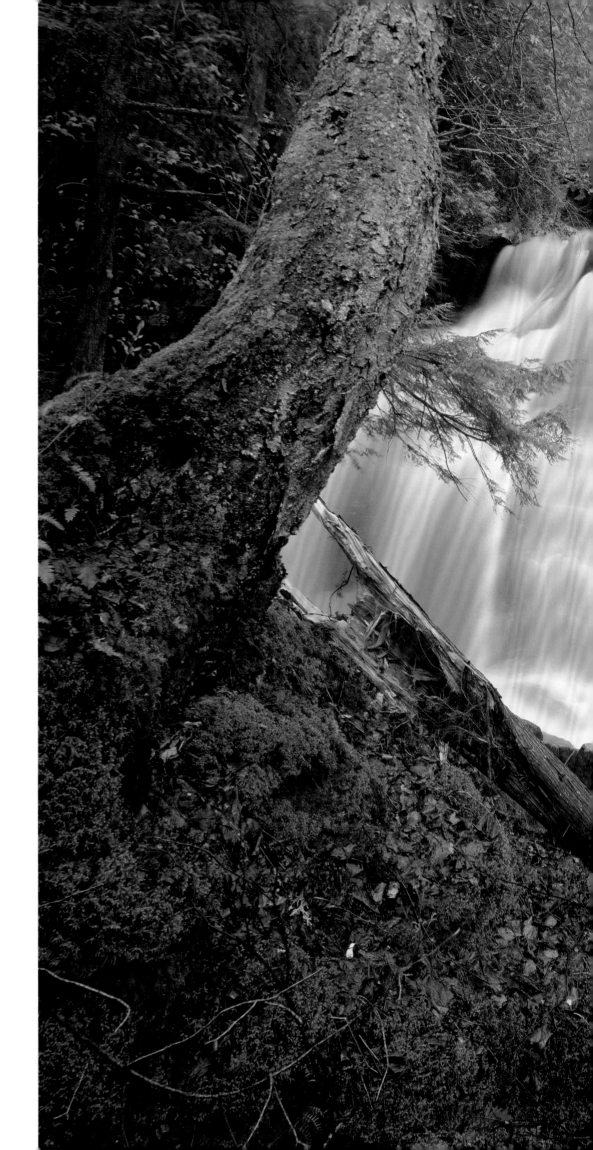

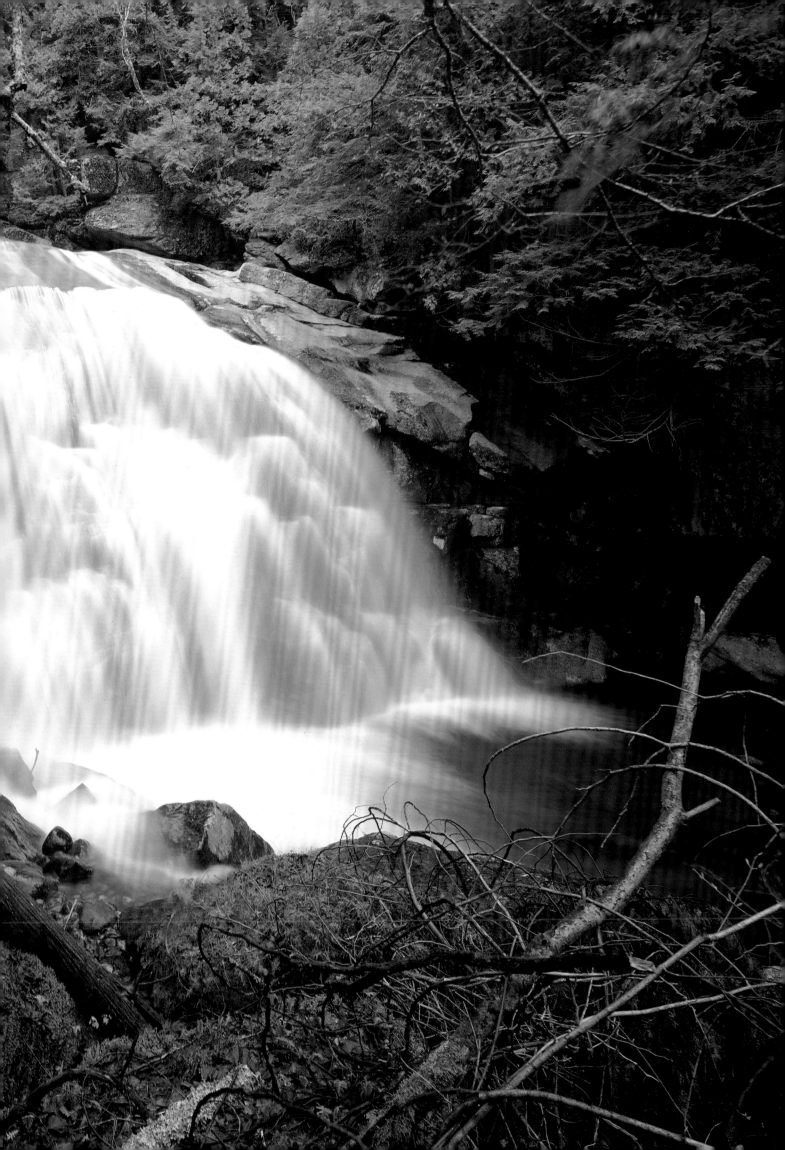

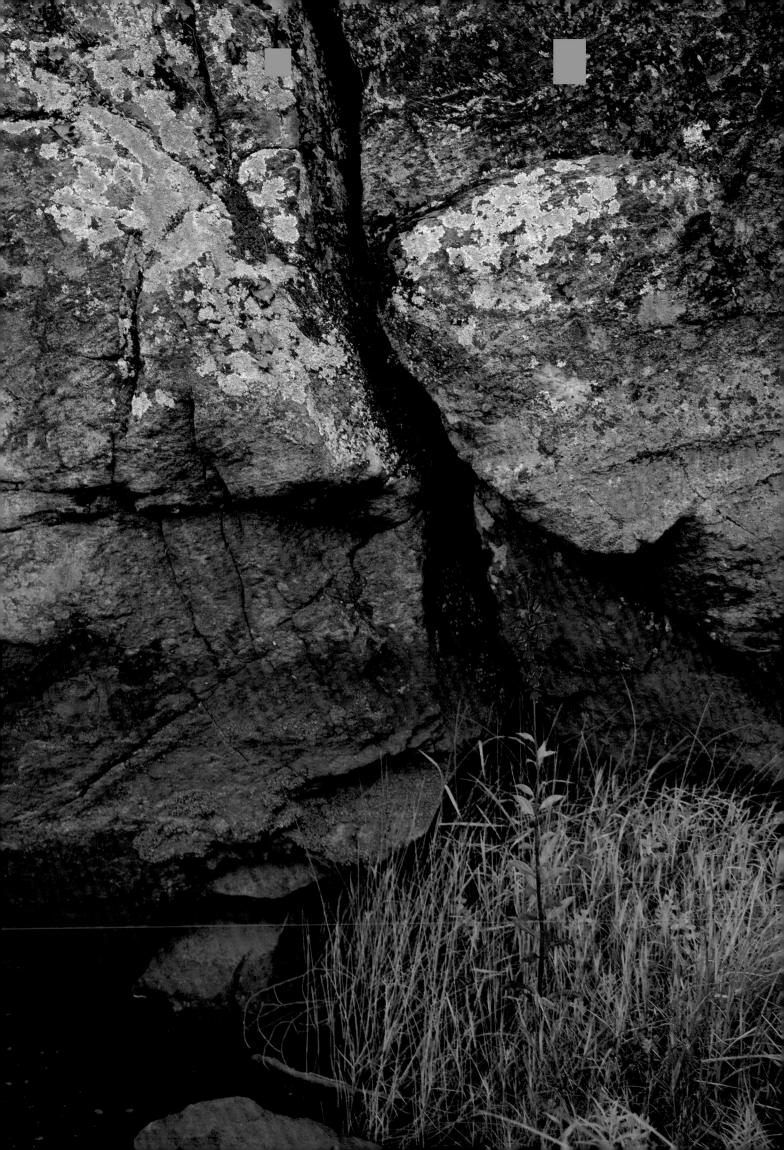

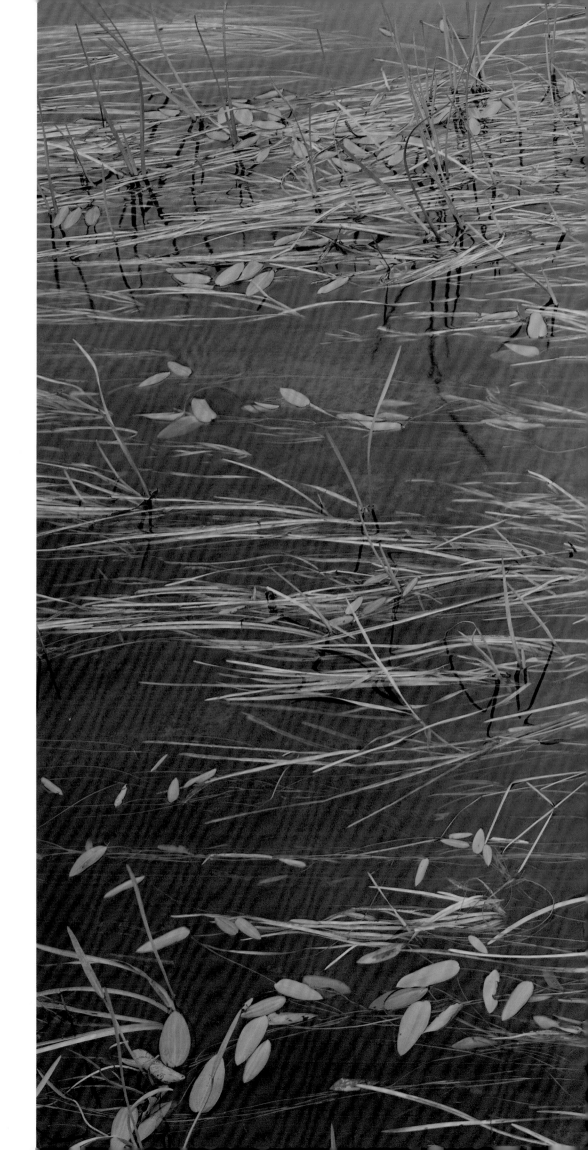

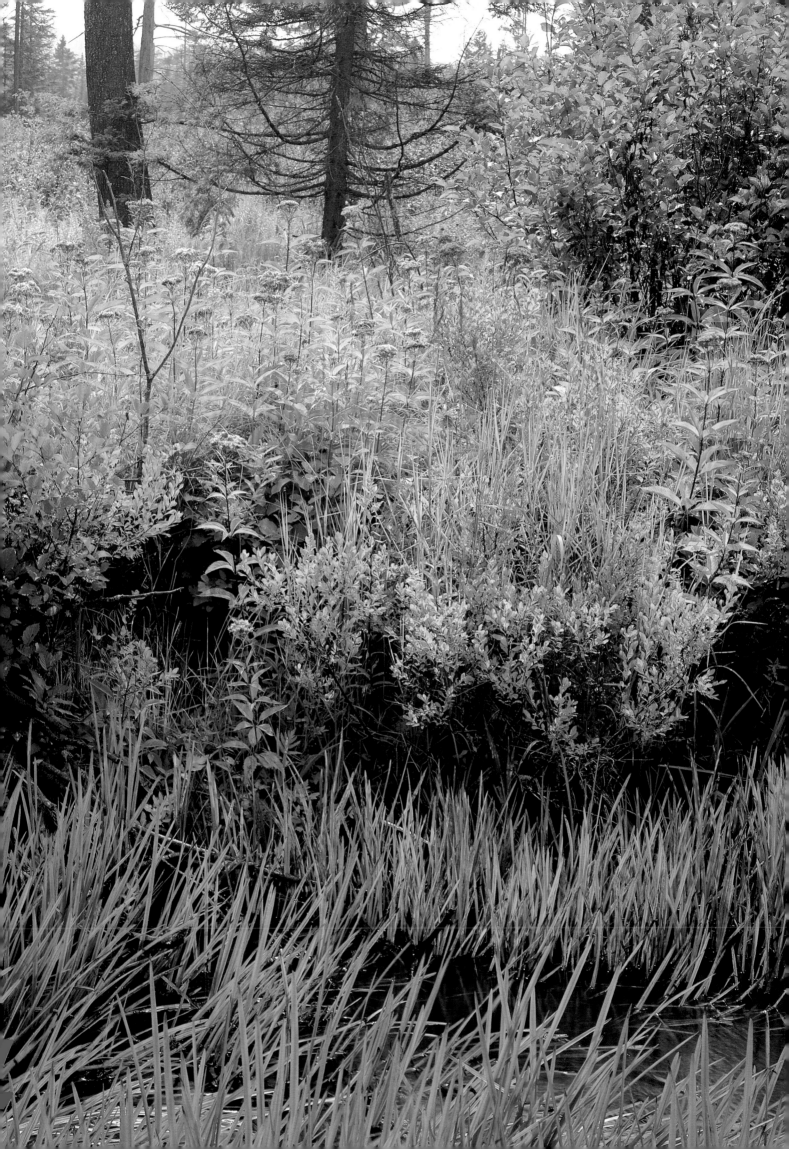

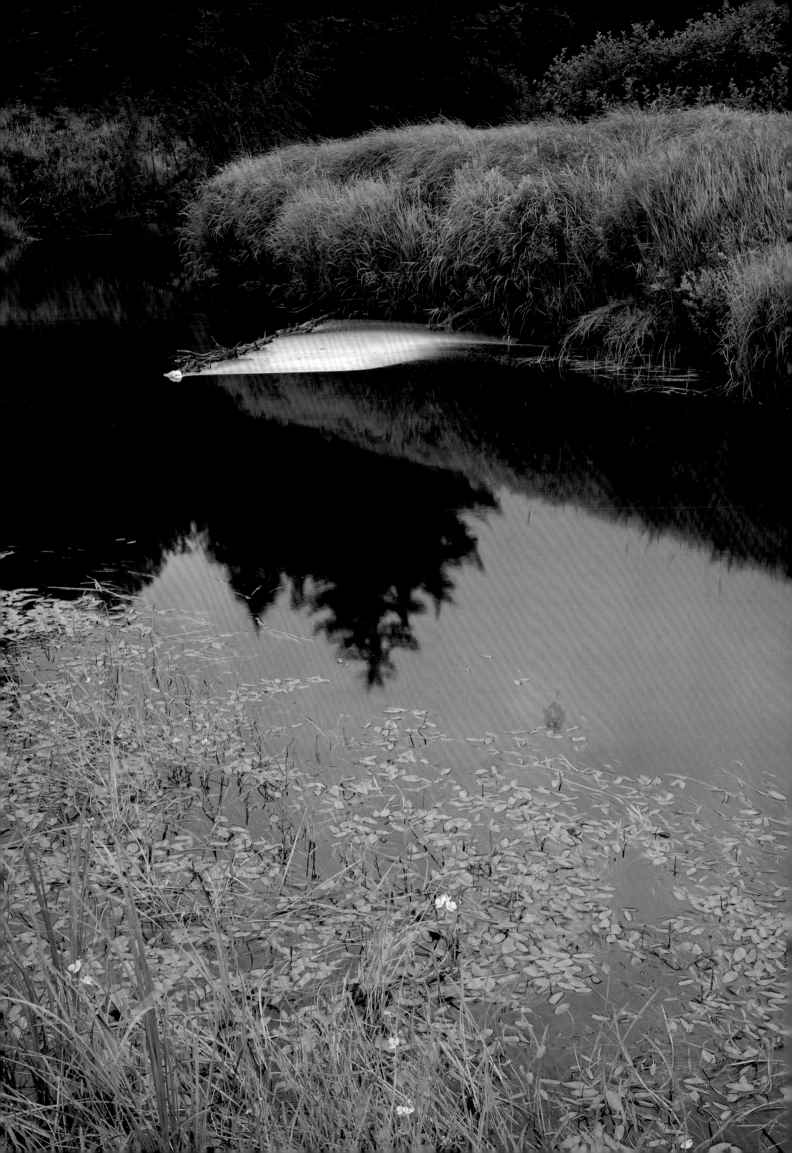

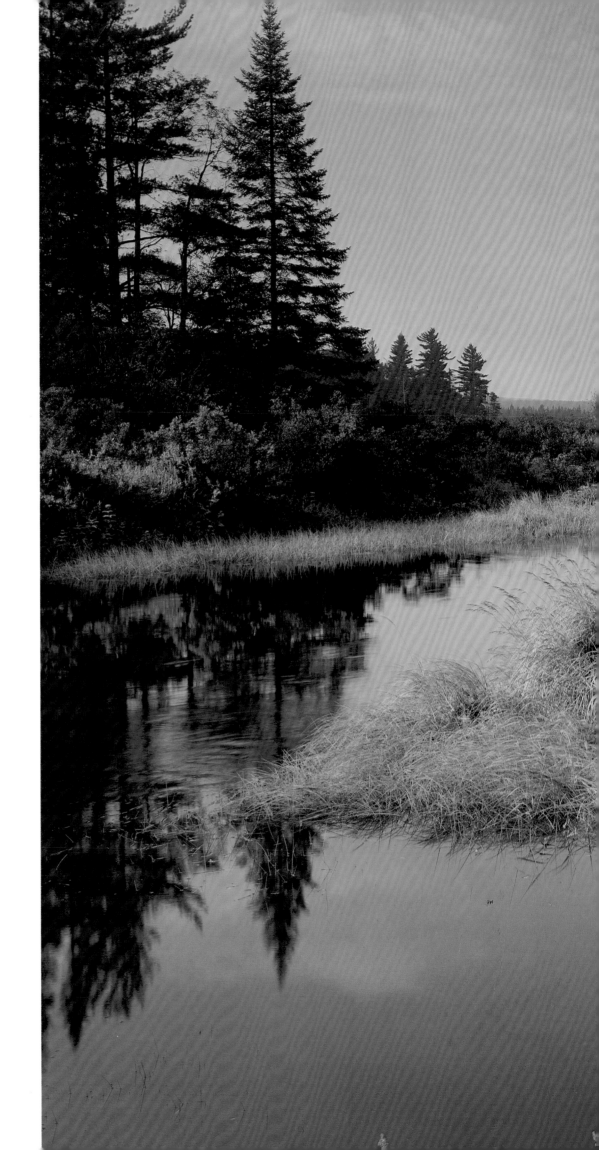

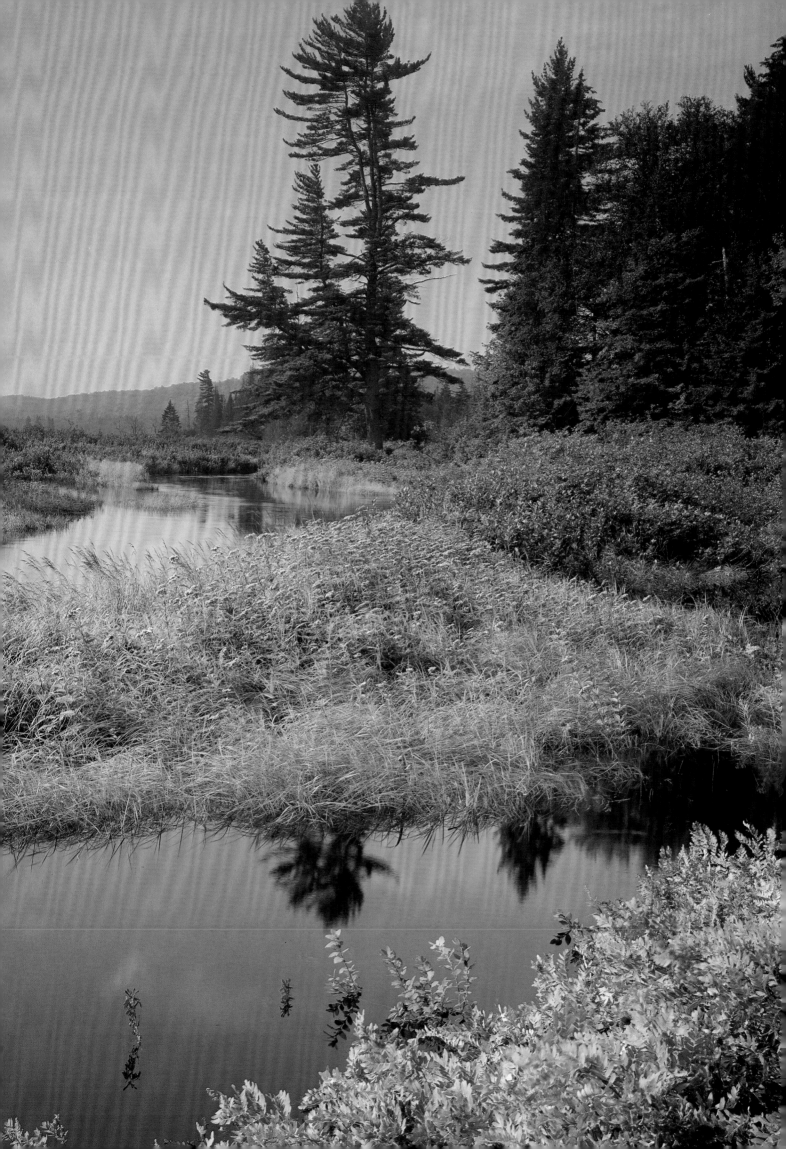

From the Mountain Tops

I had climbed alone to the summit of Algonquin in the early morning hours, arriving at the summit ahead of the sun. The night before I had slept near the four thousand foot level and risen with the predawn light. Mist enveloped me and my camera, and a swift wind was pushing at my back. I faced Mount Marcy but could not see it. I had no indication that in ten minutes, when the first rays of the sun would melt the rugged edge of Gothics, I would witness an extraordinary and spectacular natural event, Ulloa's Rings.

On the crest, twenty to thirty mile per hour westerlies were blowing, and they temporarily moved the mist off the summit to give me a glimpse of Marcy across Avalanche Pass. I walked to the leeward side trying to protect my camera from the wind, hoping that the mist would clear further so that I could photograph the sunrise. While I was setting up, the wind brought in a fresh sea of fine mist. With wet air swirling around me and zero visibility, I walked the few yards back to the summit to see if I could get any idea when this would blow over. It did. Then the mist came back again, and cleared again. Each time I looked to the west, I saw a new wall of white moisture moving toward me. As I looked at one of those impending white walls, the sun rose behind me and I saw an enormous circular rainbow on the newest sheet of moisture. I stood amazed. I played with my glasses, thinking that they were acting as a prism, but when I put them in my pocket the rainbow remained. When I put them back on, I saw that my gray shadow was projected into the center of the circles of color. Then, as fast as it had happened, the mist that had acted as the projection screen for this great show moved in and enveloped me, and the image slipped out of focus.

Pages 58–59: The Great Range from the First Brother

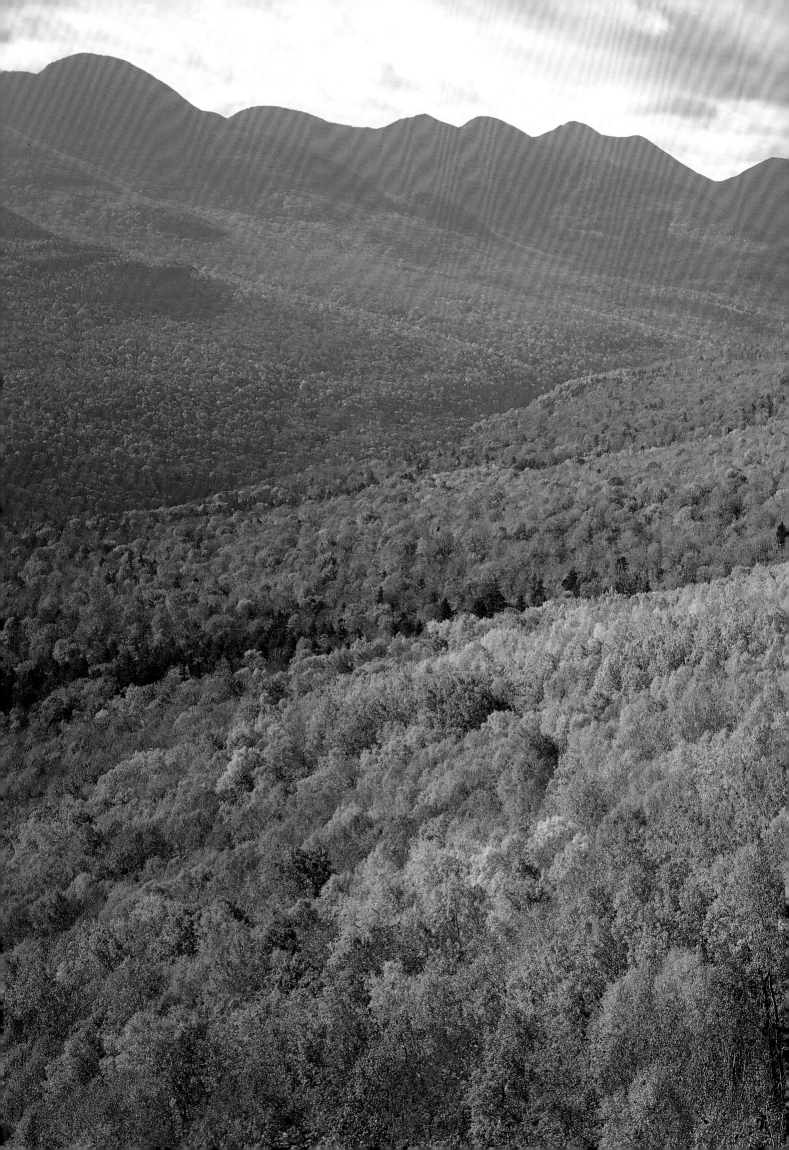

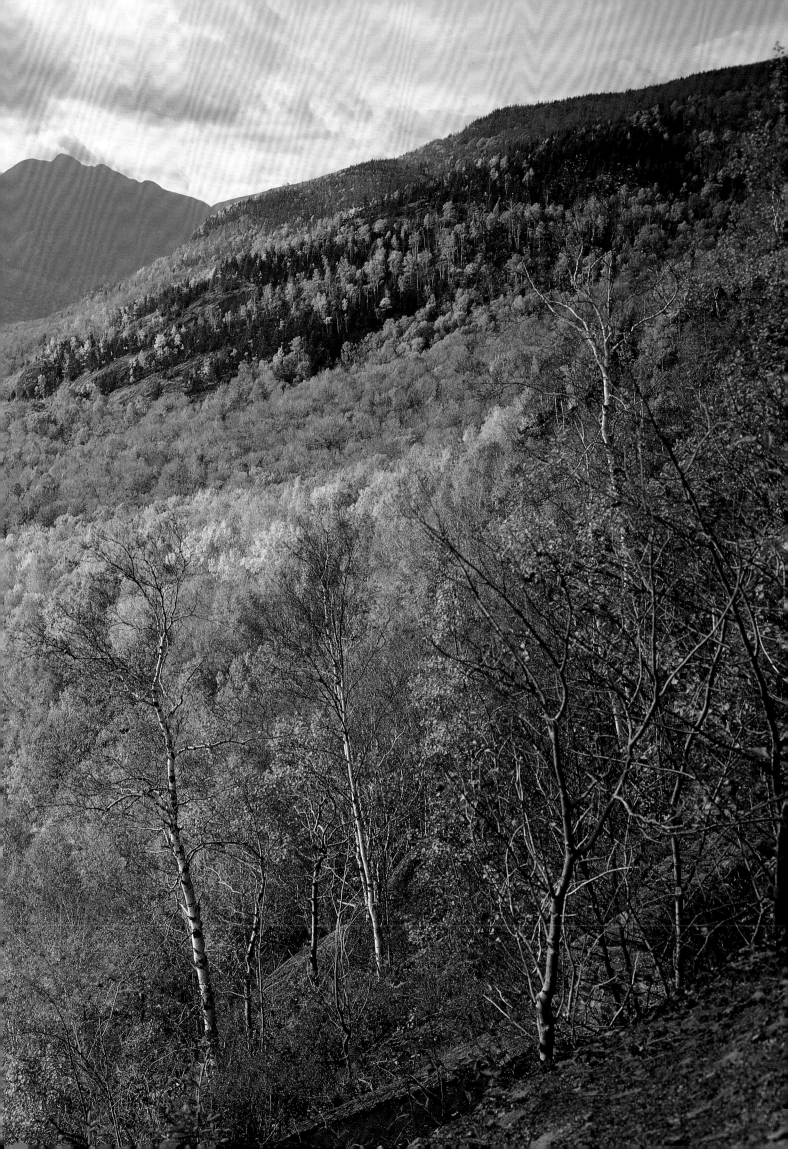

Within a few weeks I met John Fritzinger, a knowledgeable Adirondacker, who took me to his home and showed me Verplanck Colvin's detailed drawing of this rare phenomenon called Ulloa's rings. Every climb cannot provide such magic, but each ascent is still exhilarating. The mysterious light that diffused the air when I took the photograph from the top of The Brothers was remarkable in its own way. Old Mountain Phelps was right. Being on top of these mountains is very close to being in heaven.

Page 61: Alpine meadow on Algonquin

Pages 62–63: View from Balanced Rock on Pitchoff Mountain

Pages 64–65: Rocks at Wolfjaw Brook

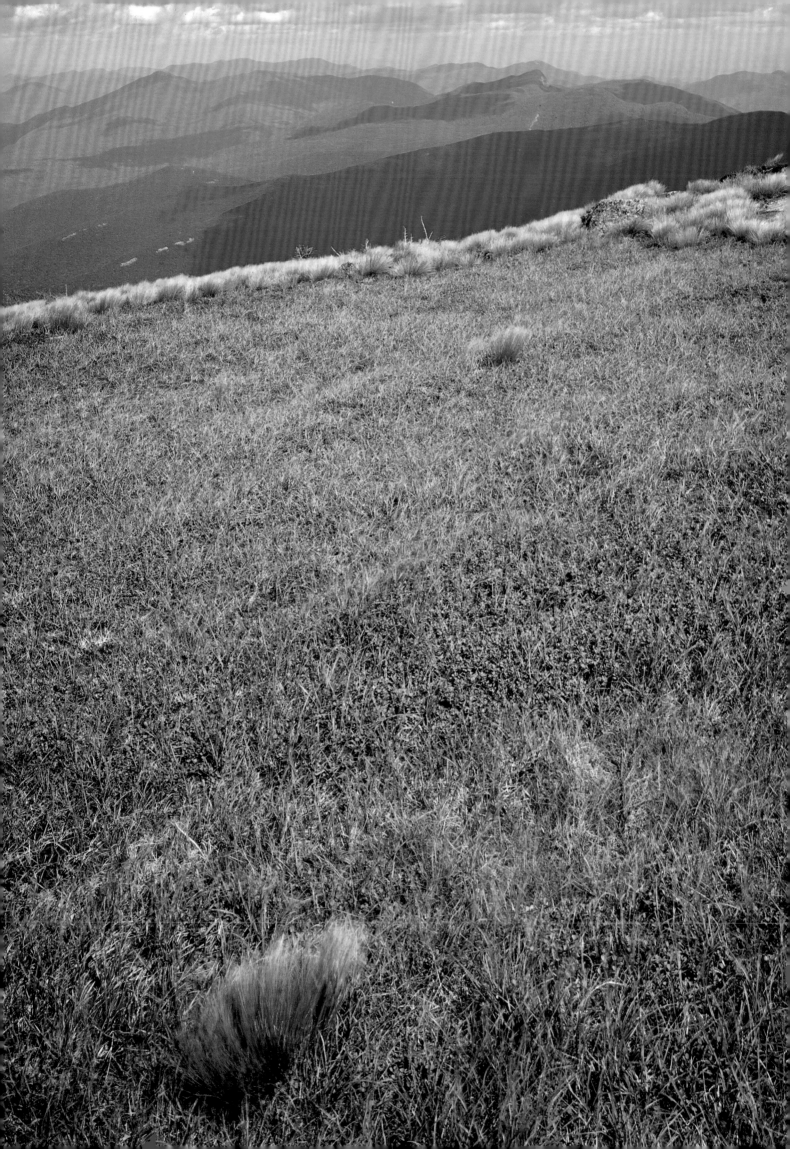

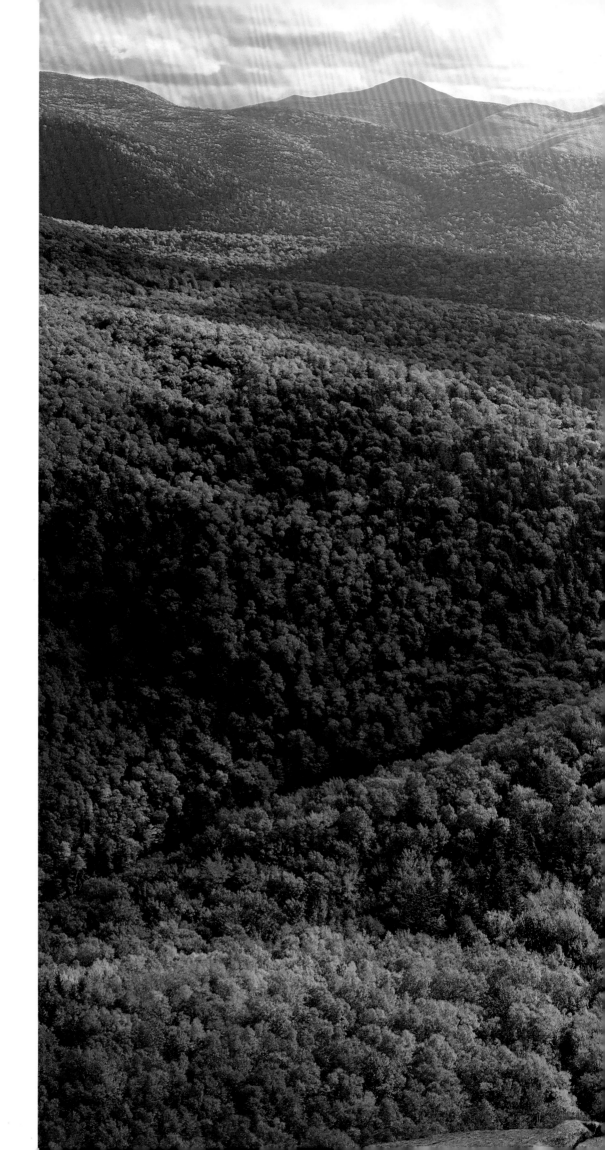

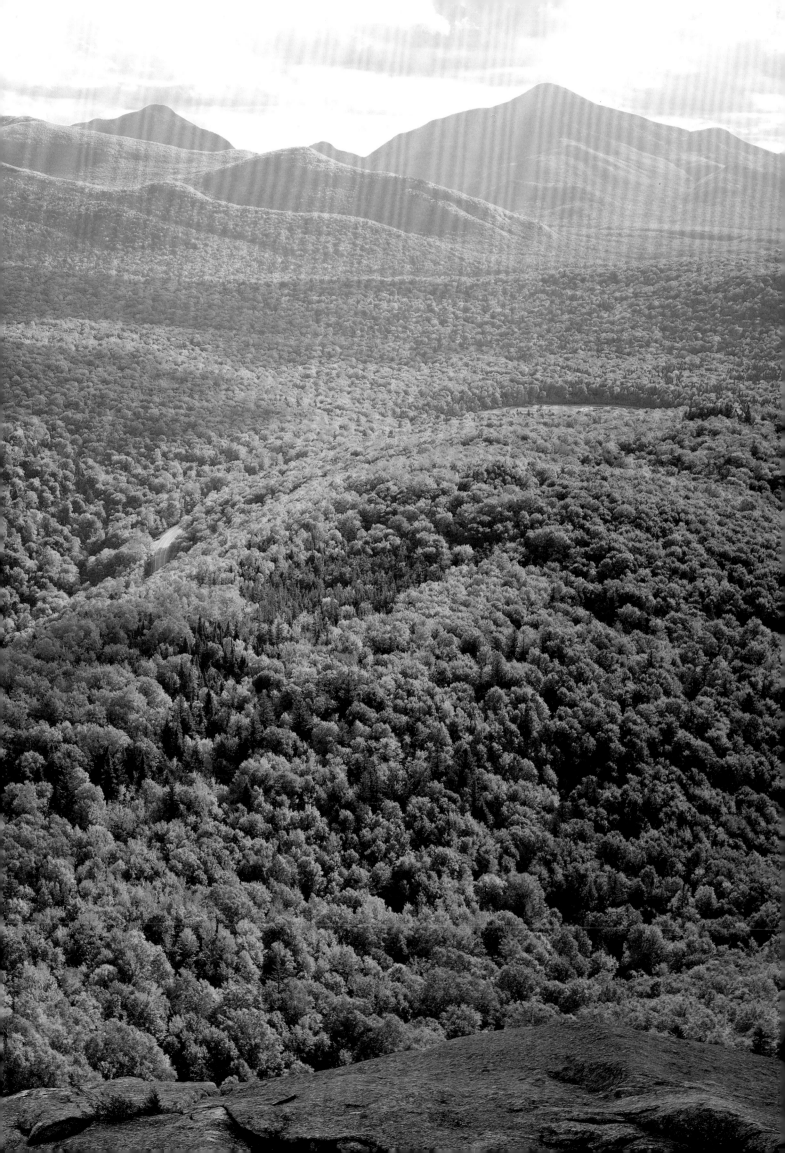

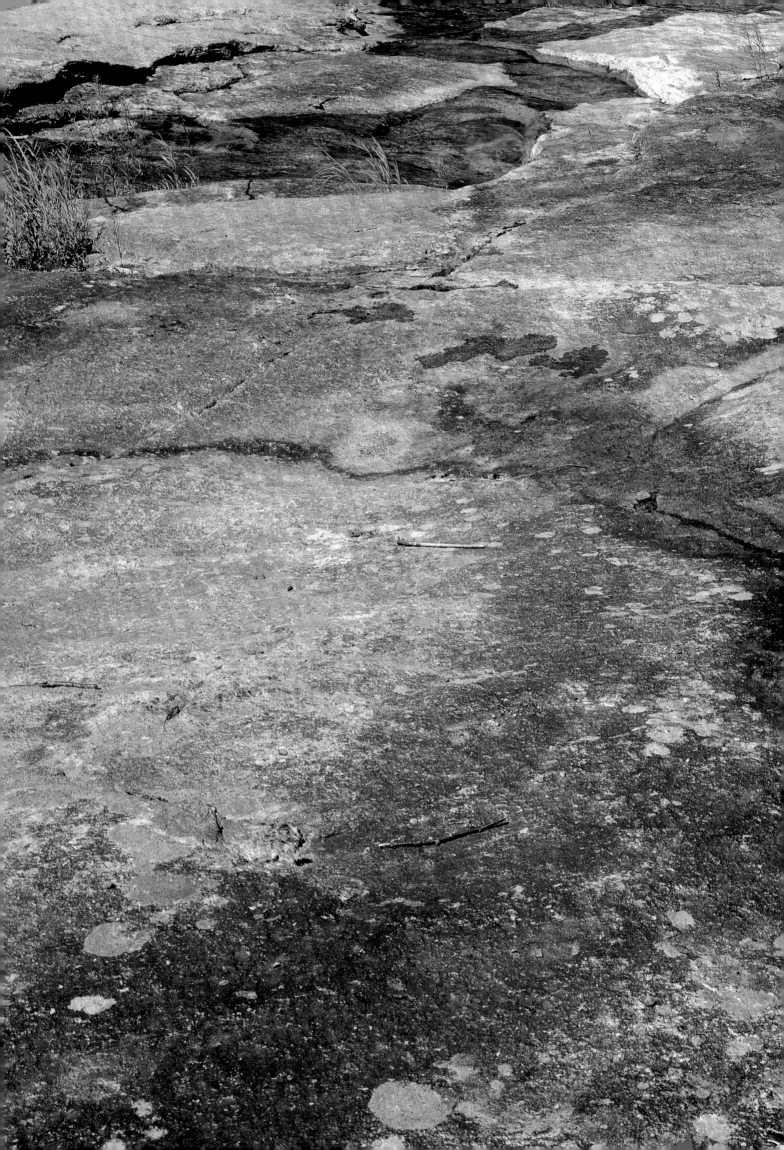

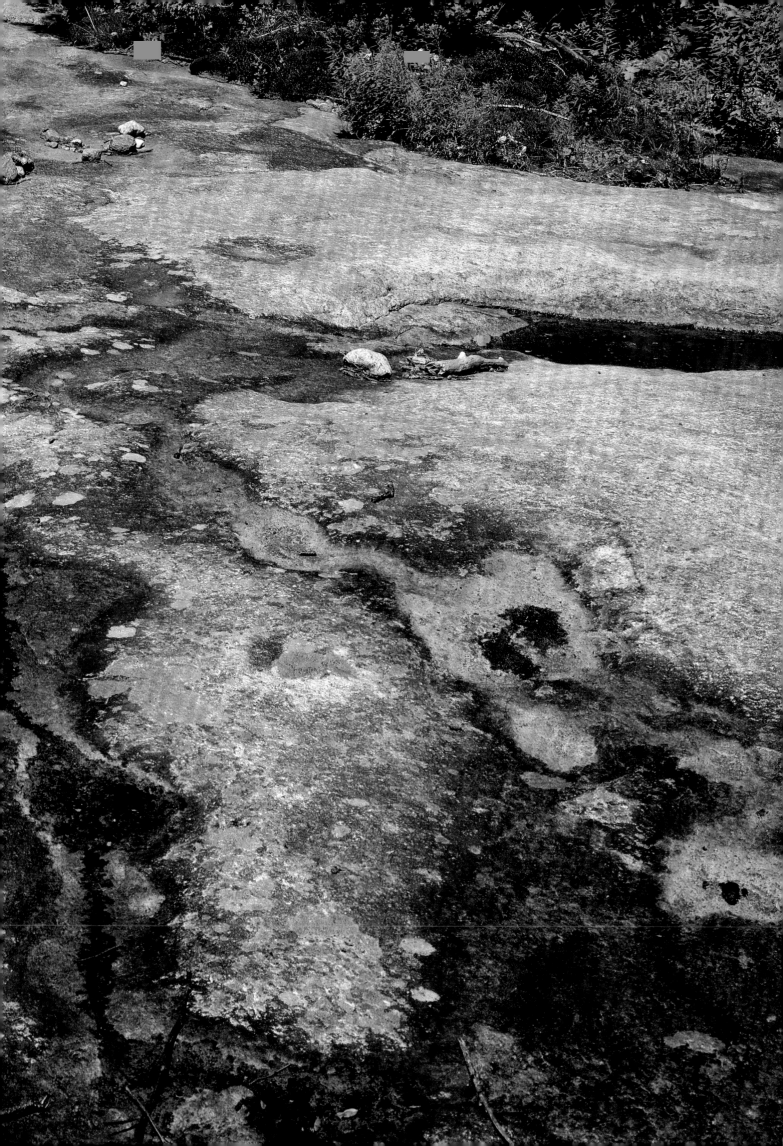

Page 67: Mount Marcy and Mount Colden from Algonquin

Pages 68–69: Mount Marcy from Wright Peak

Pages 70–71: Looking east from Wright Peak

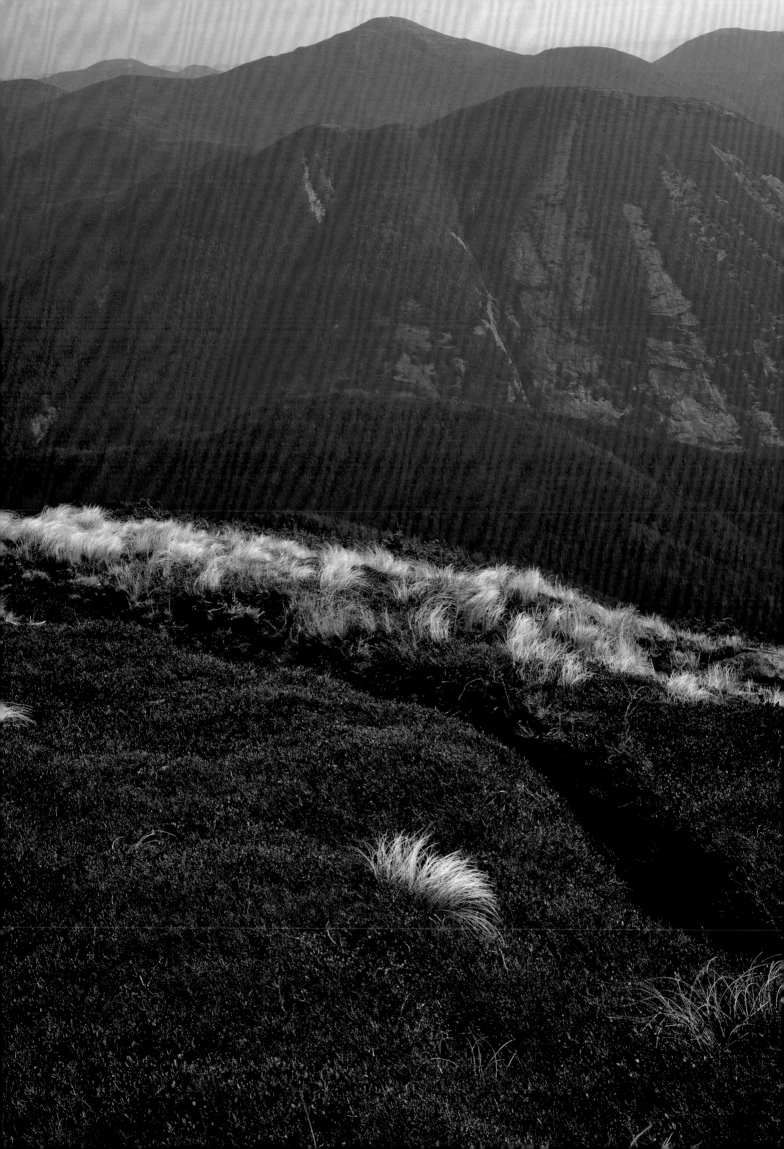

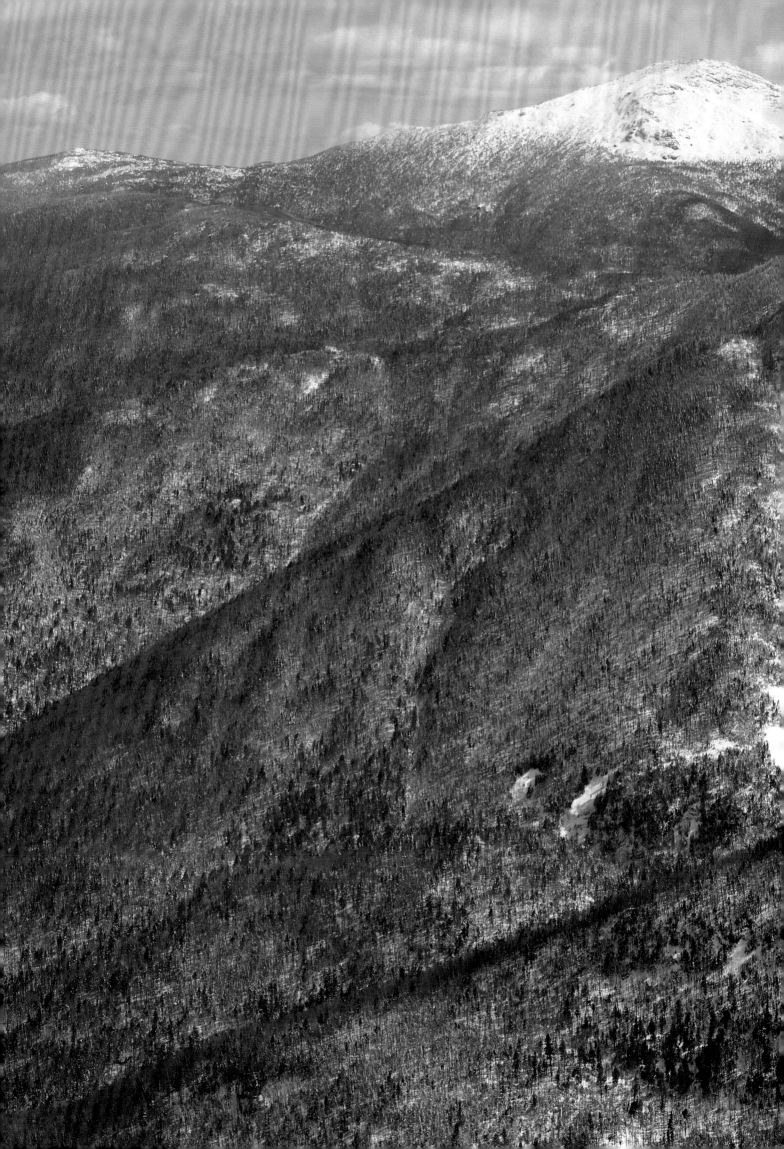

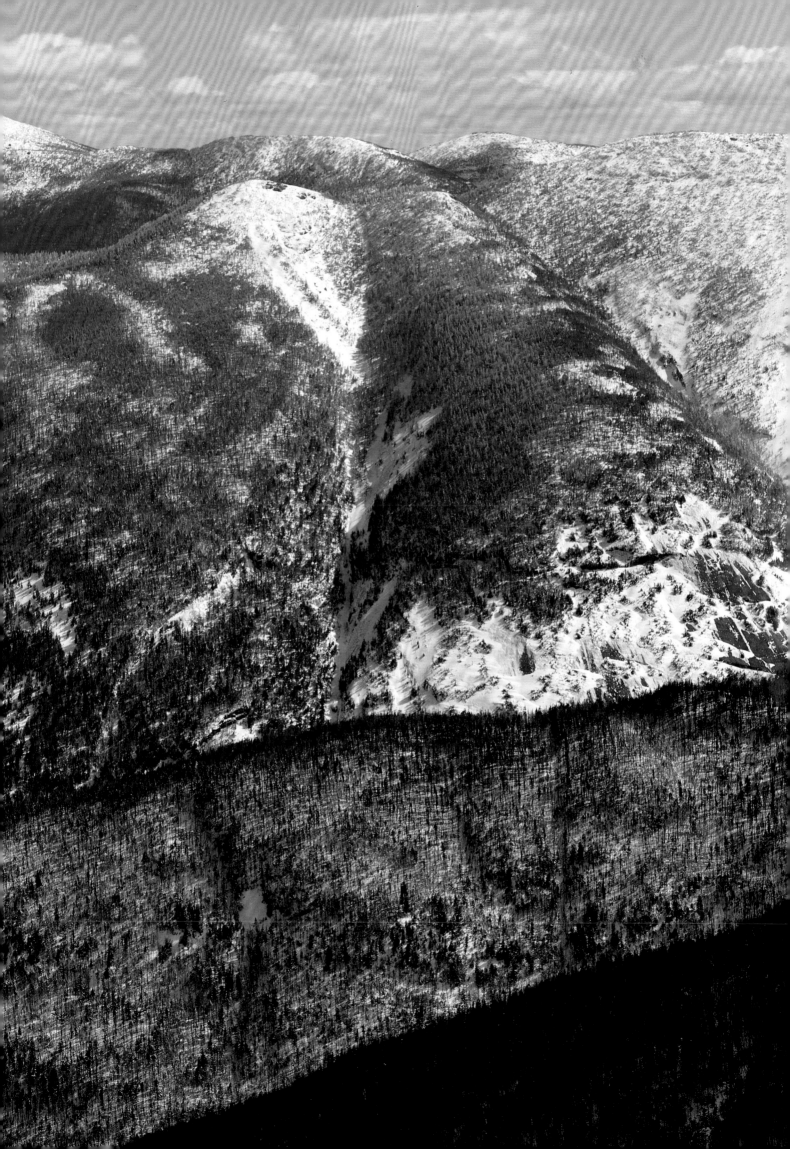

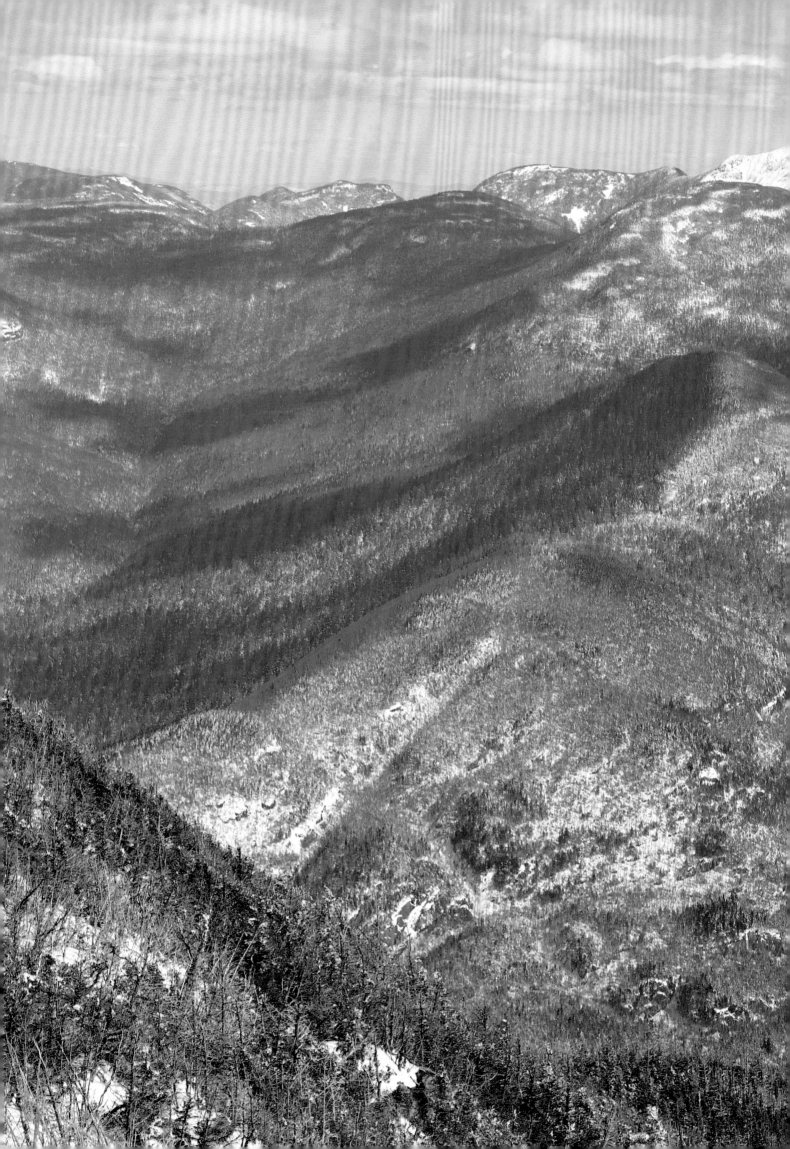

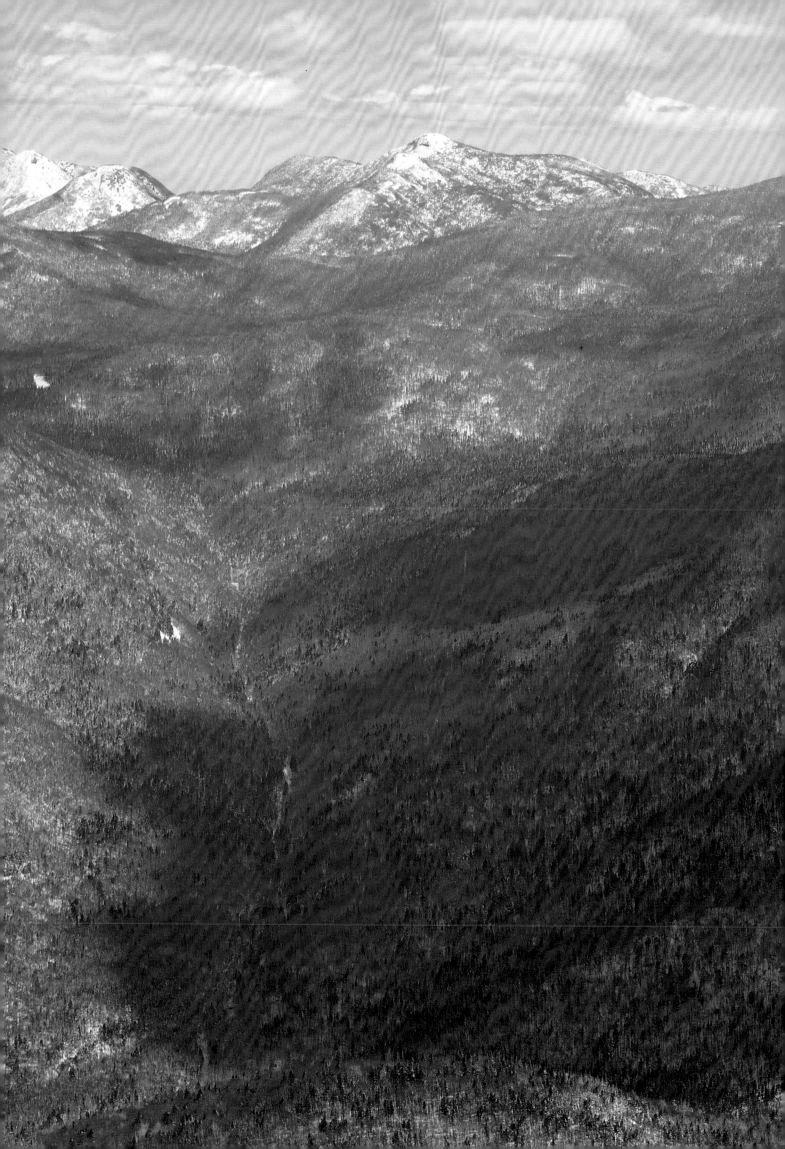

Page 73: Looking south from Mount Marcy. In this area there is an enormous number of dead spruce trees. Throughout the mountains of the northeast spruce trees have been dying at an alarming rate in the past several years. A number of scientists believe that this is due to acid rain. The Adirondacks receive more acid rain than any other region in the United States and there is almost no limestone that can act as a natural buffer.

Pages 74–75: The Mount Marcy Stillwater from the summit of Mount Marcy

Pages 76–77: View from the summit of Cascade Mountain

Pages 78–79: View south over Clear Pond from Sunrise Mountain

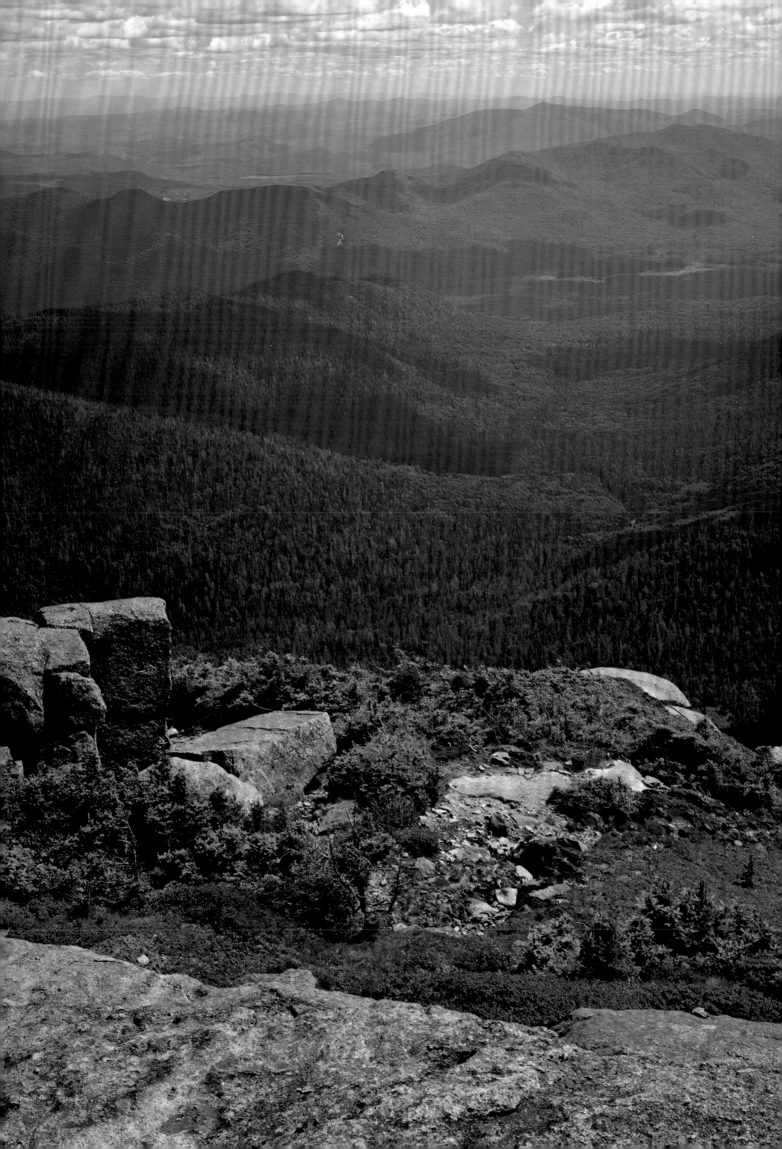

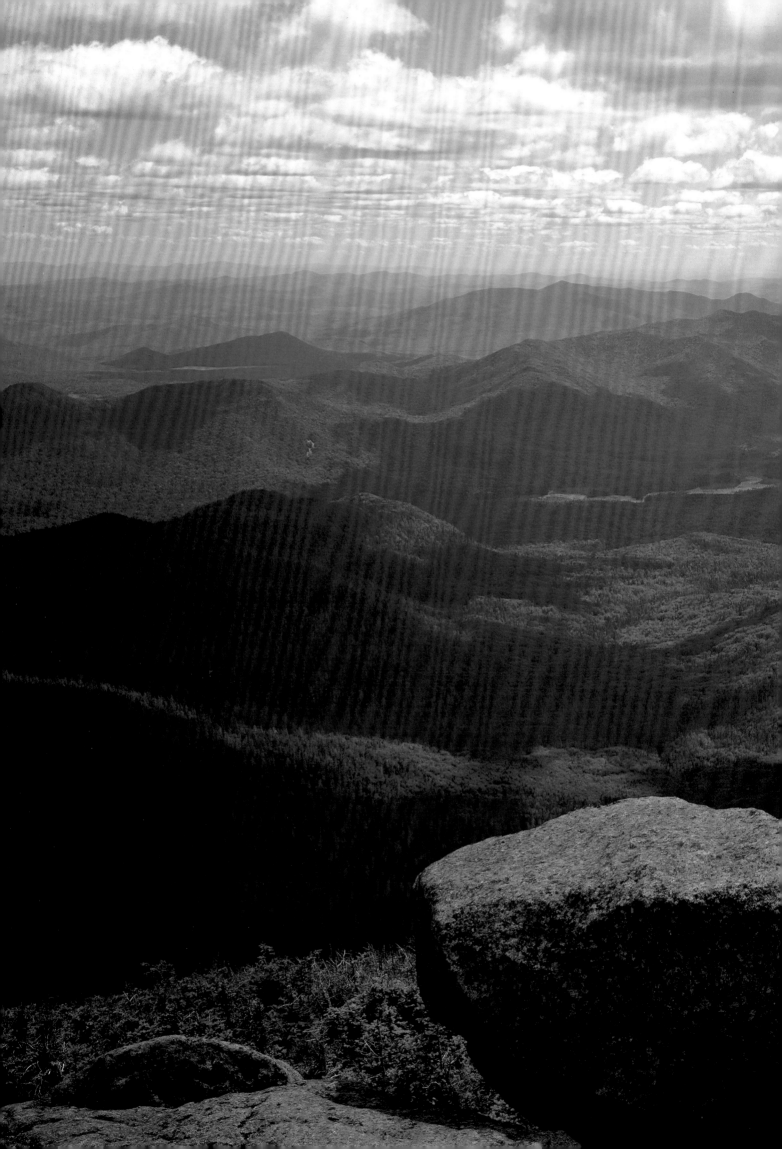

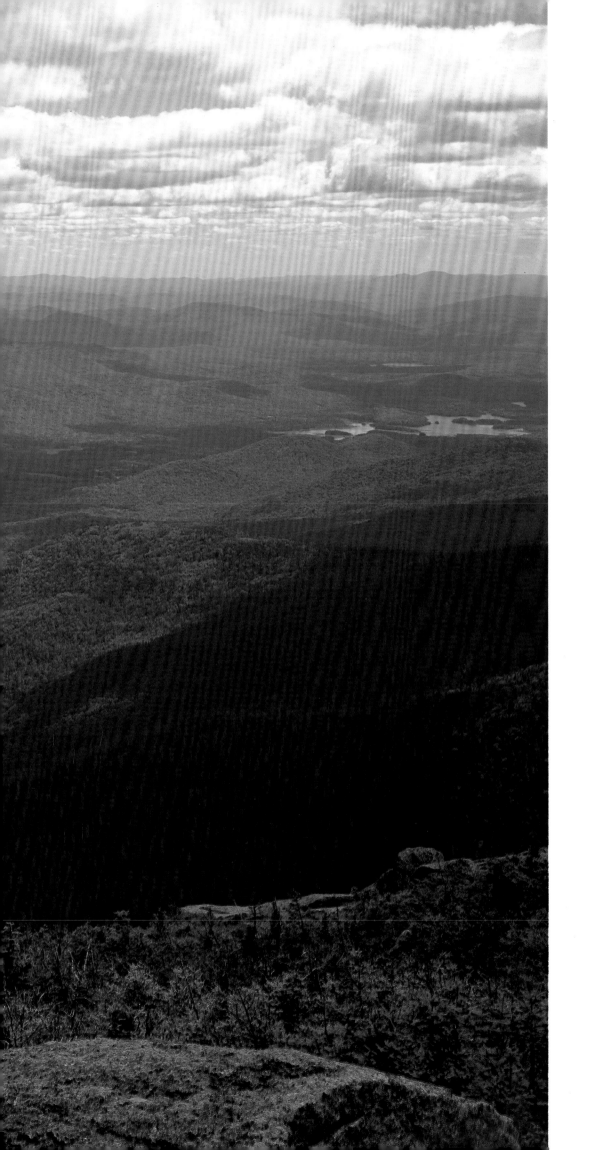

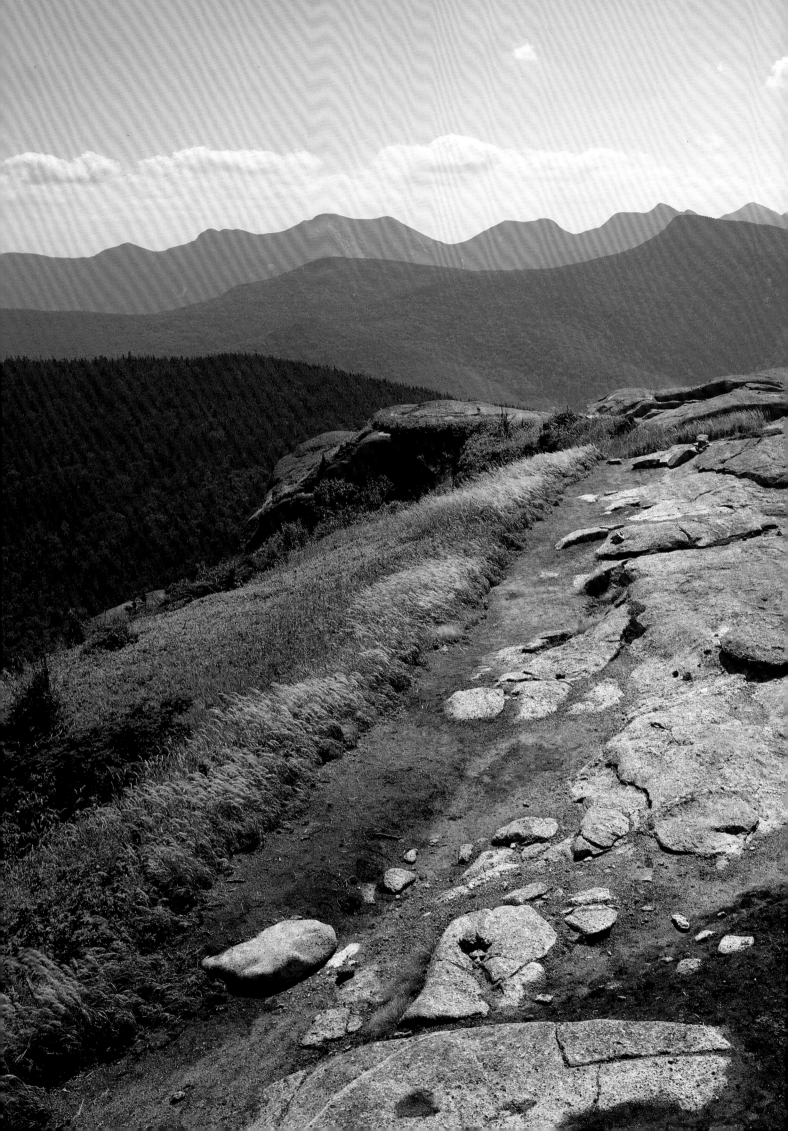

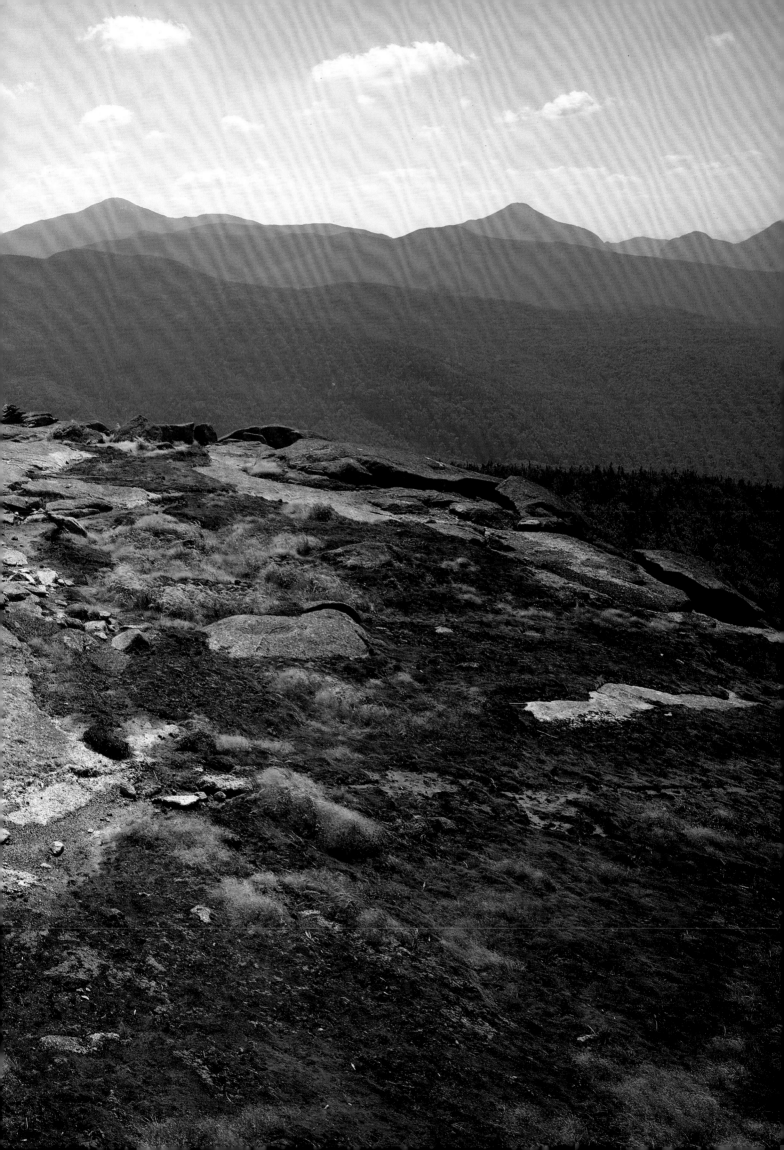

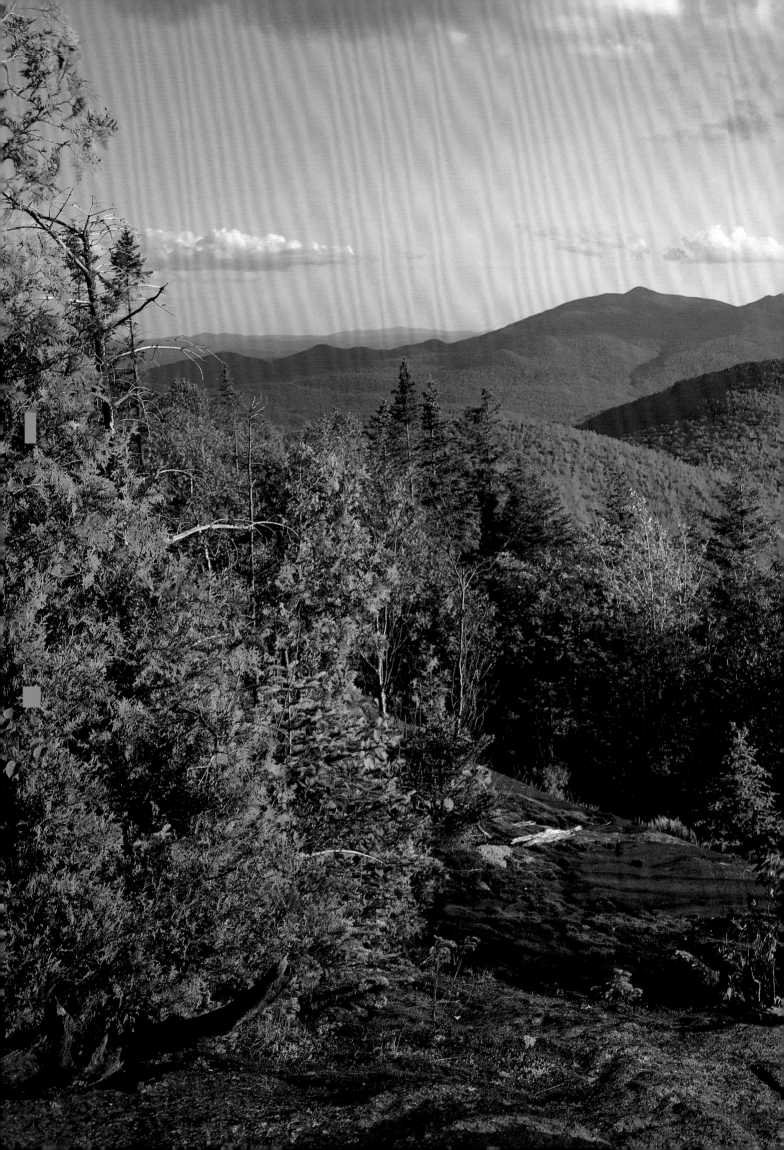

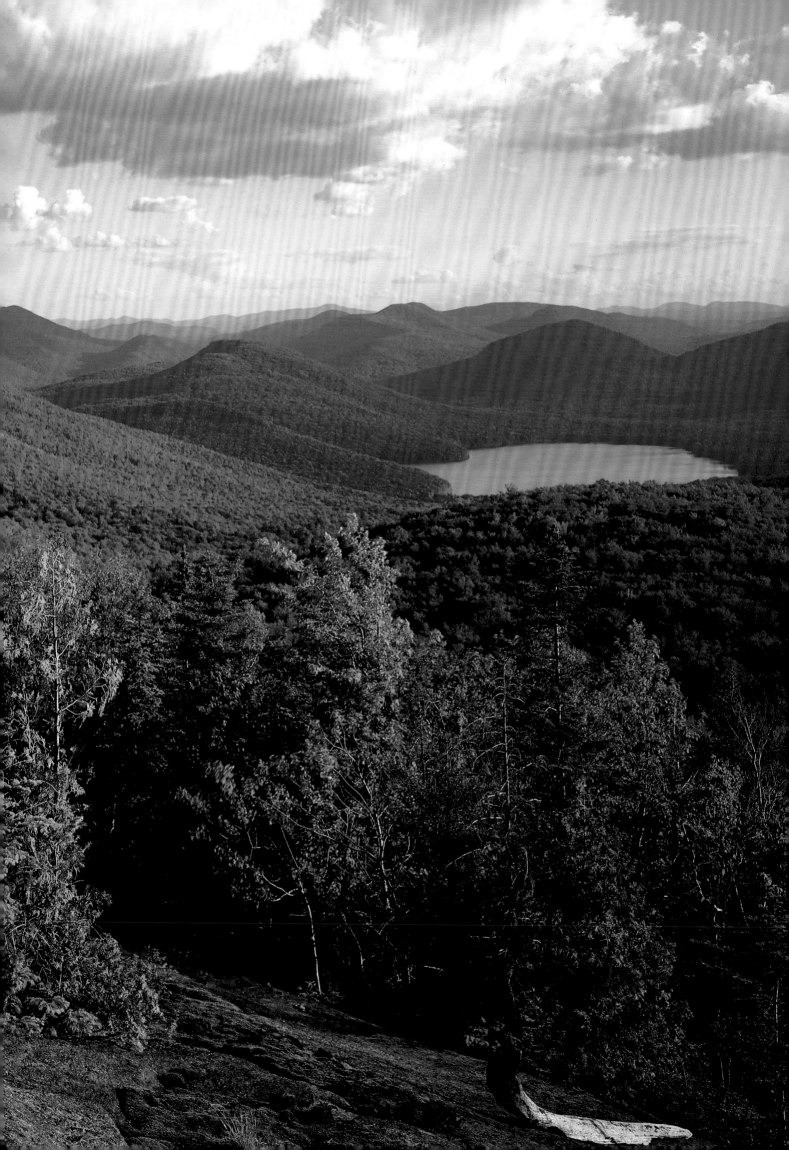

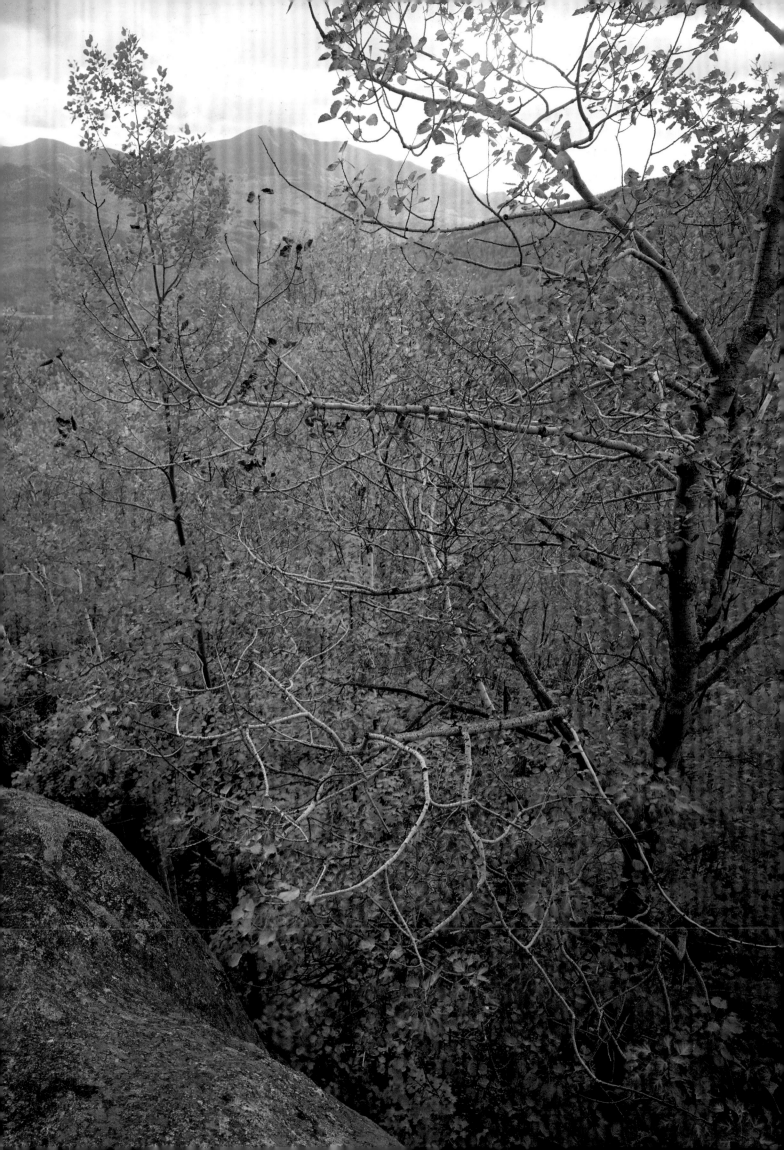

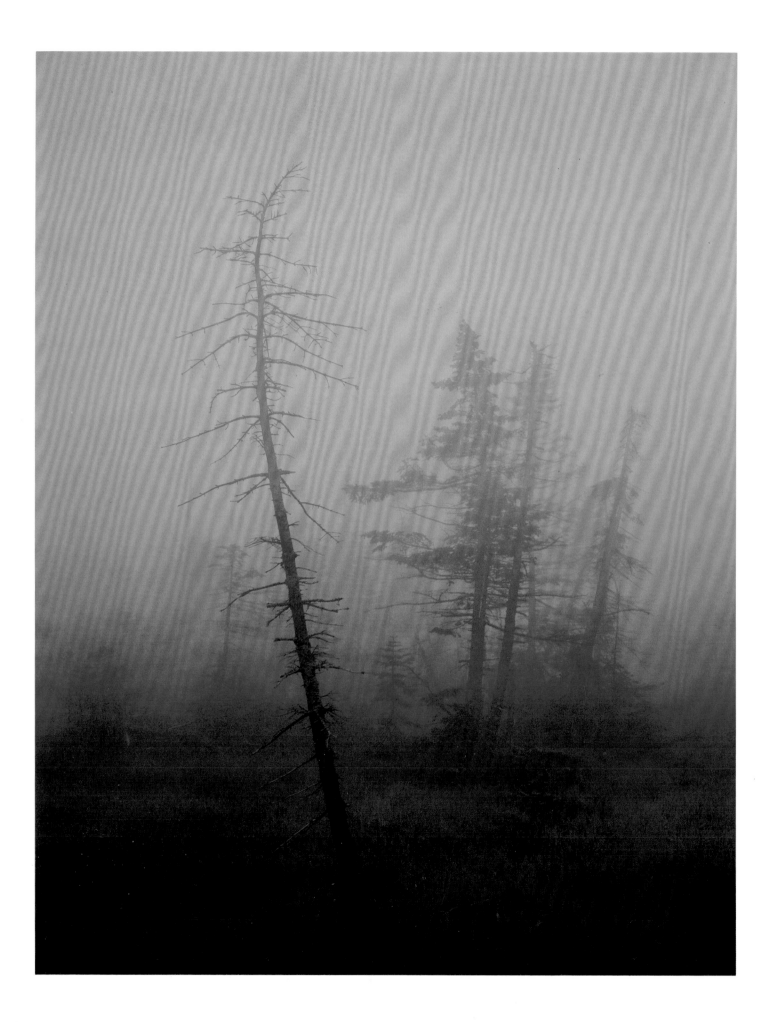

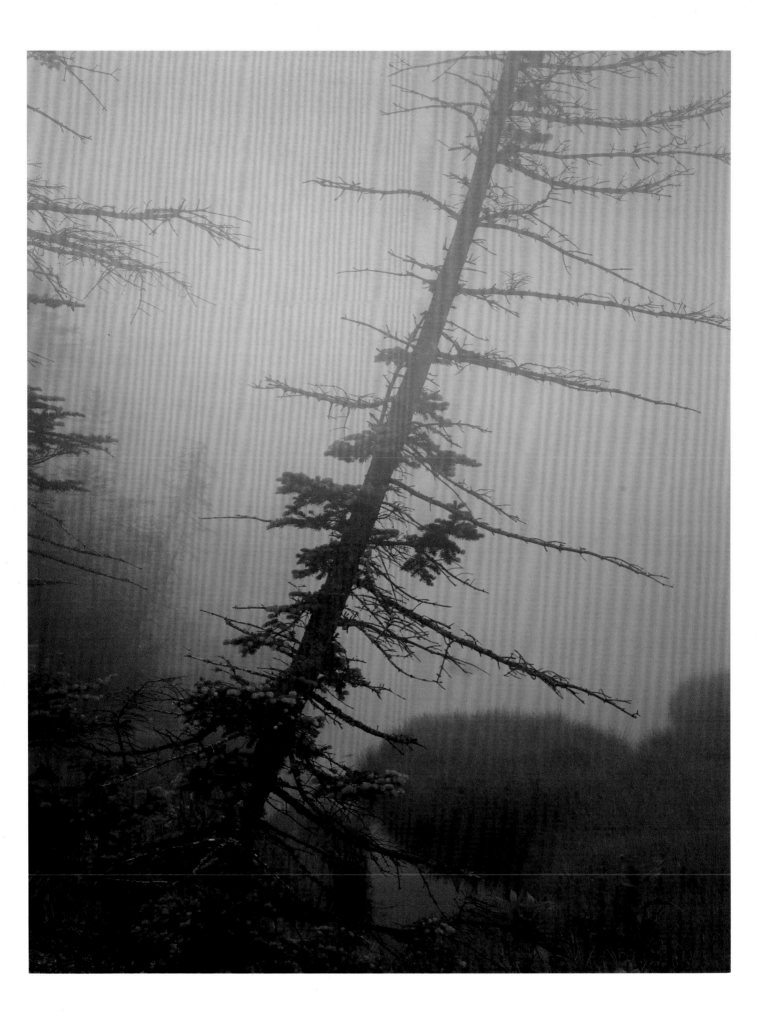

Page 85: Avalanche Pass

Pages 86–87: Basin and Big Slide from the summit of Haystack

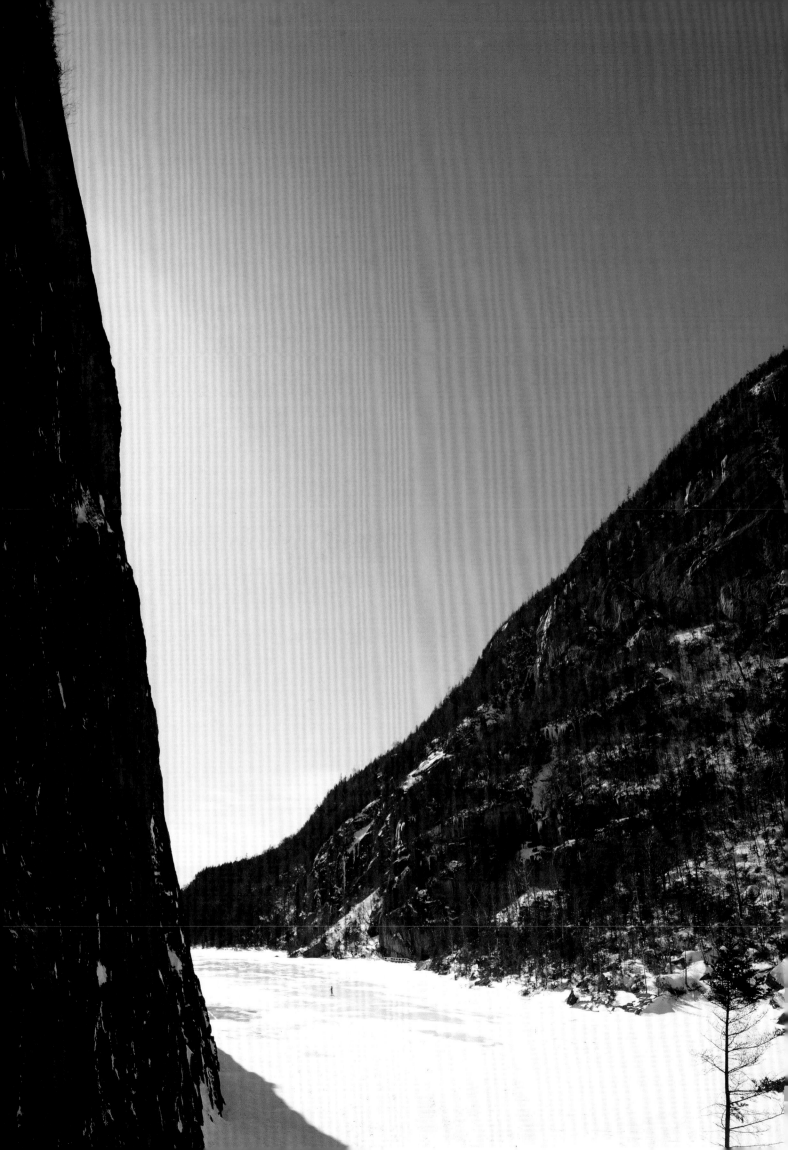

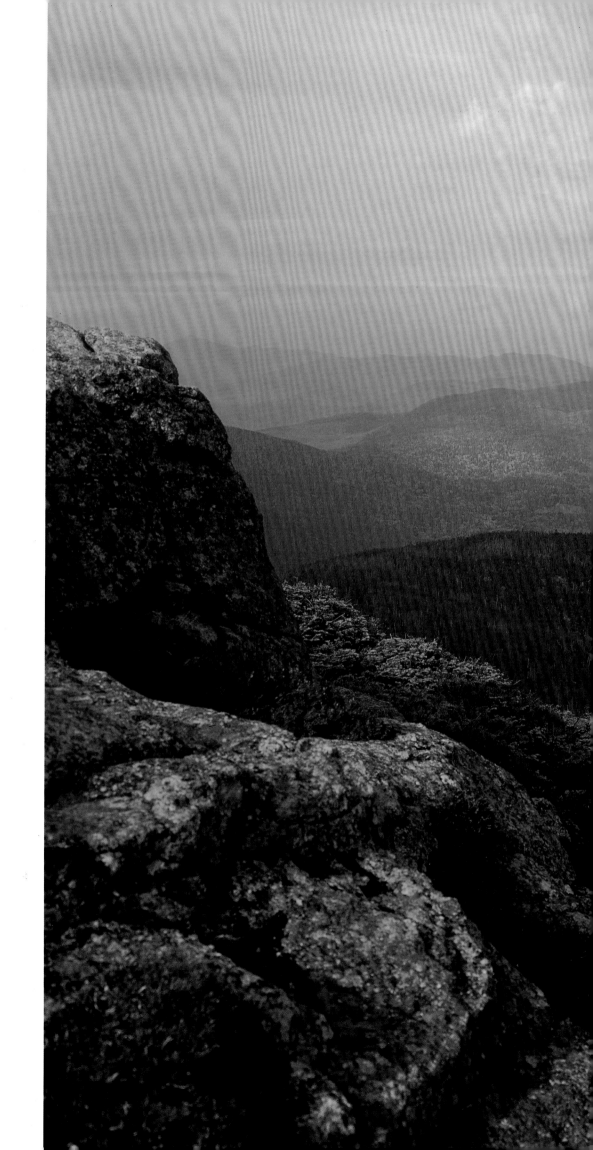

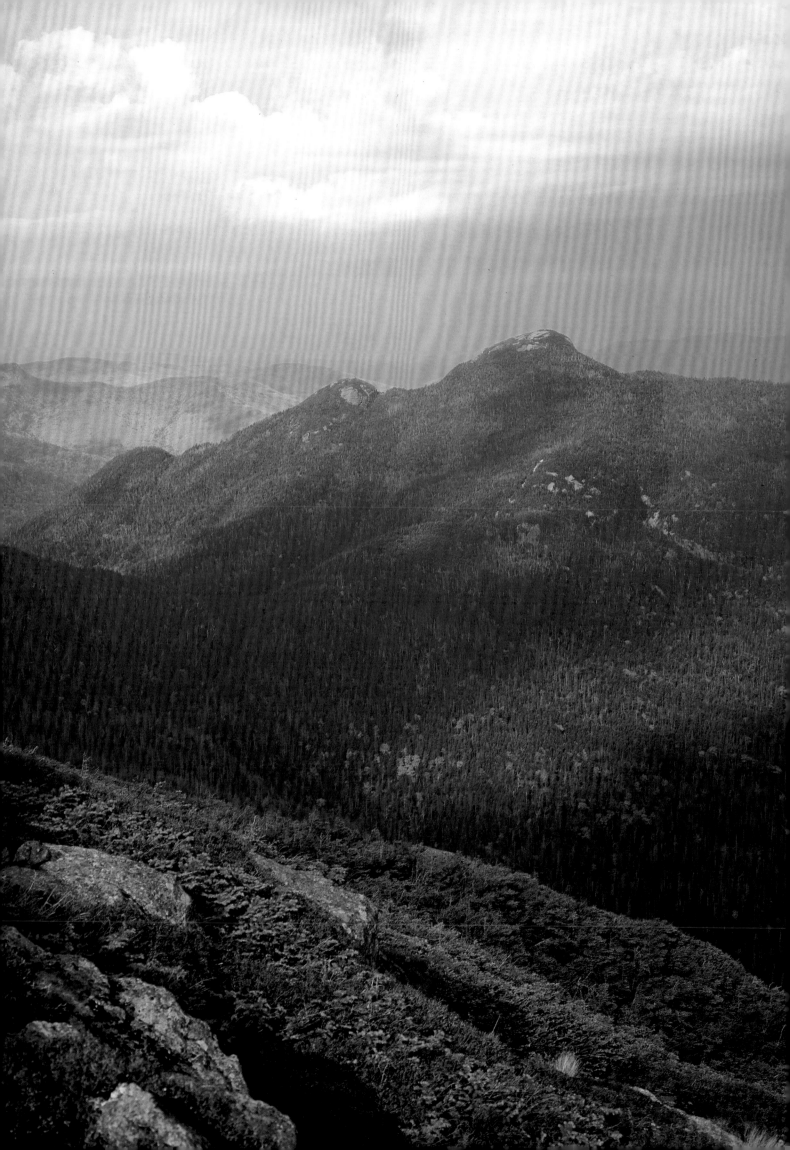

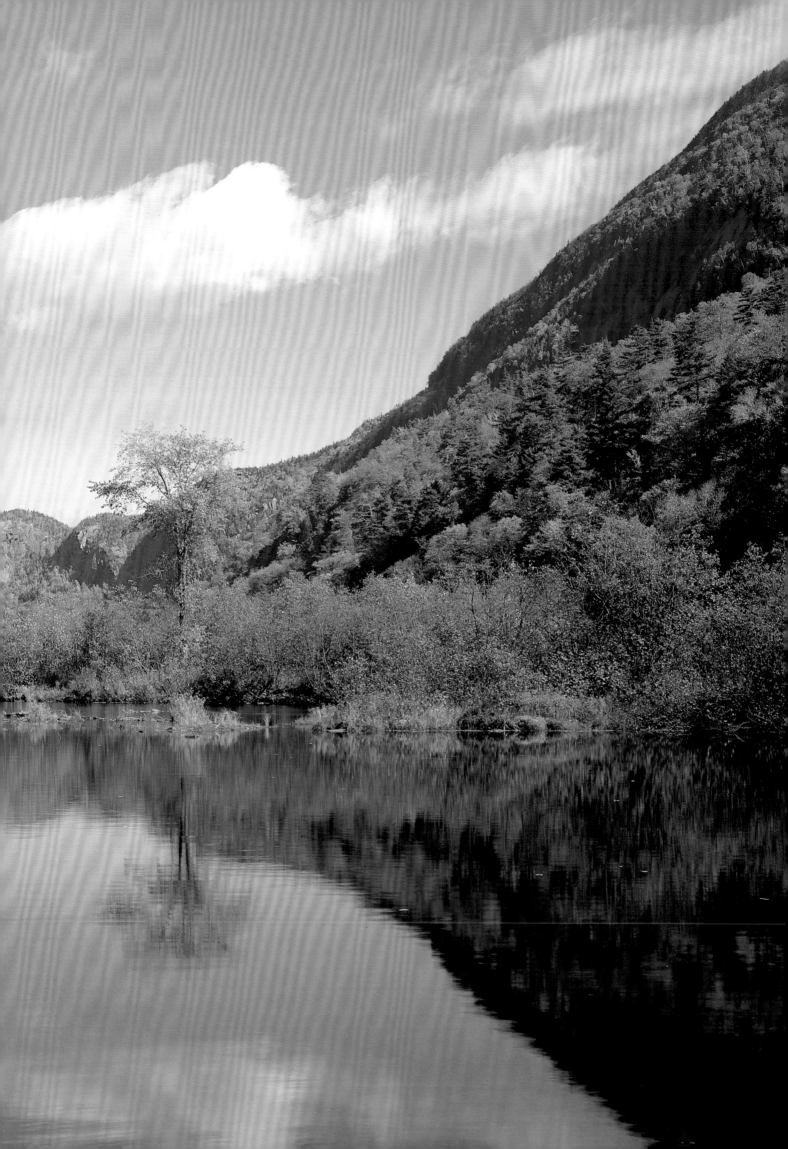

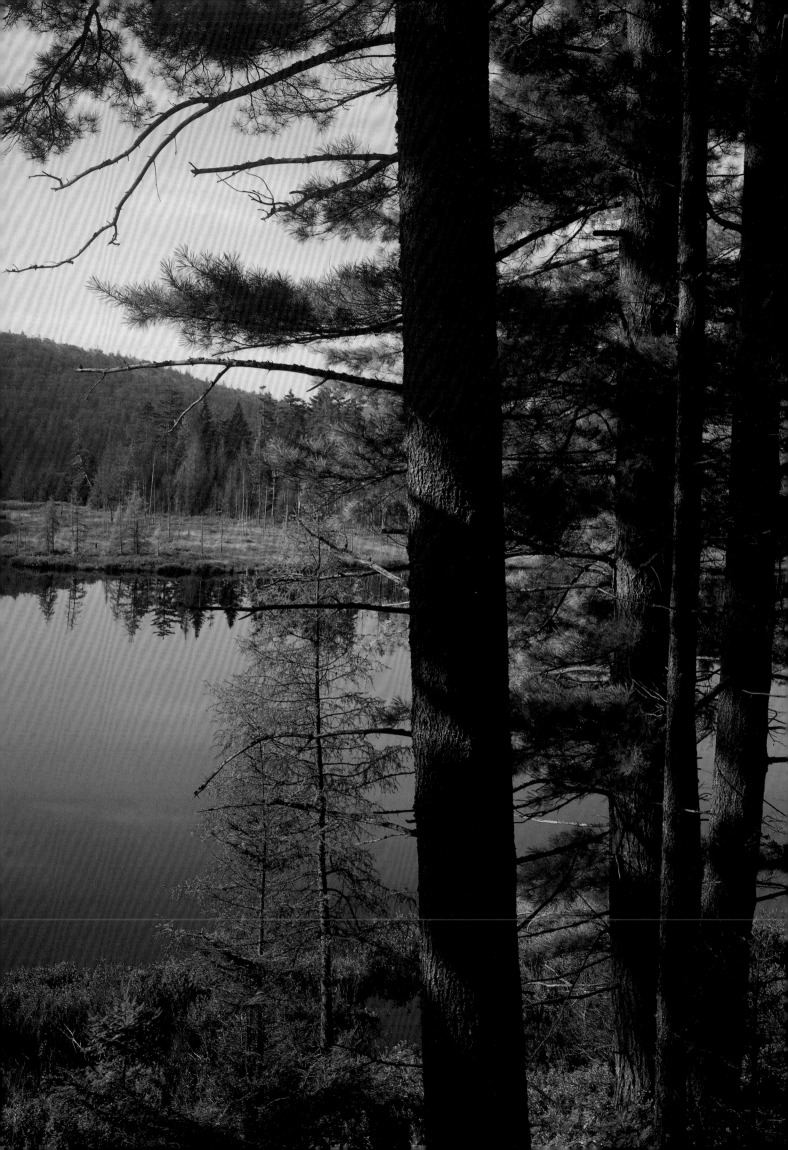

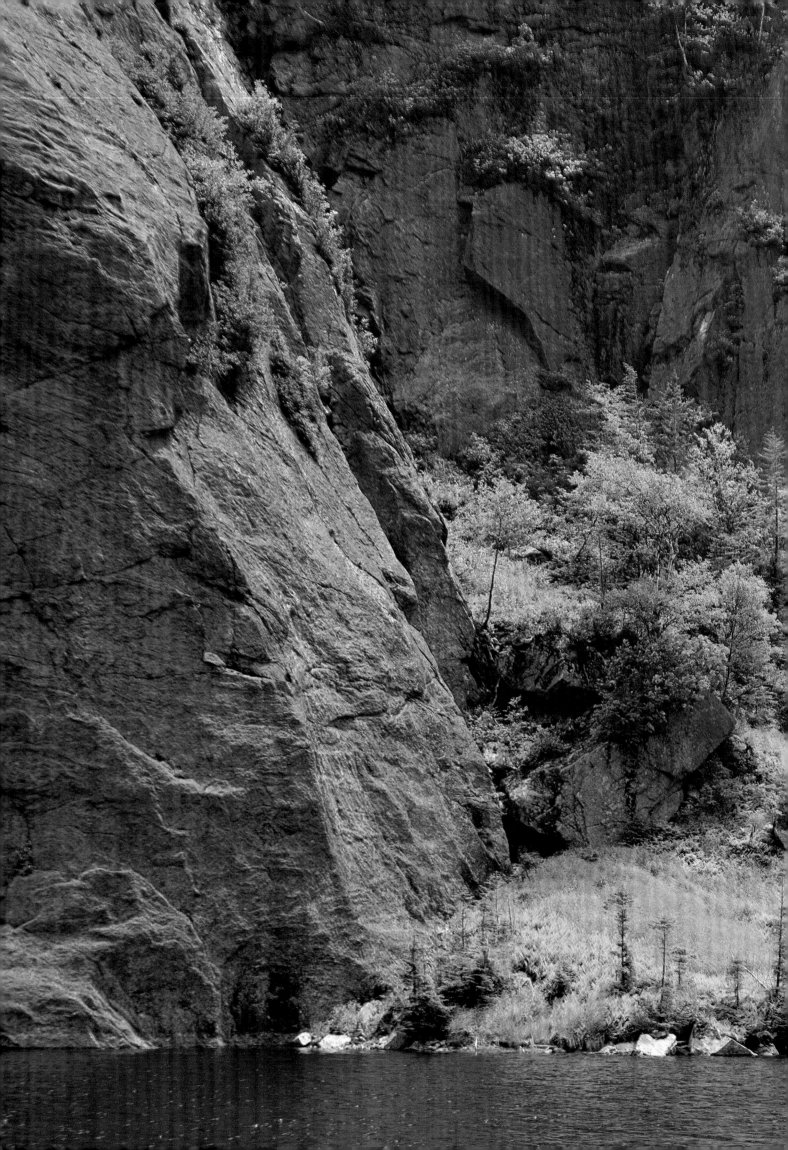

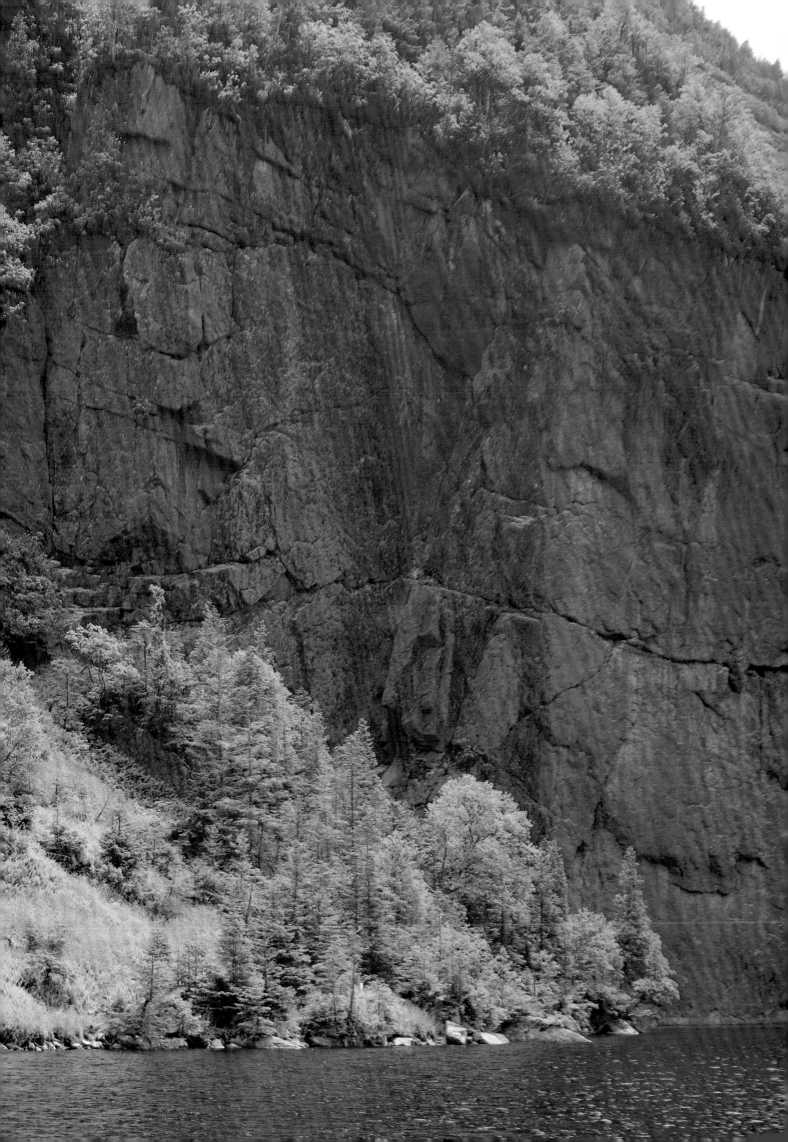

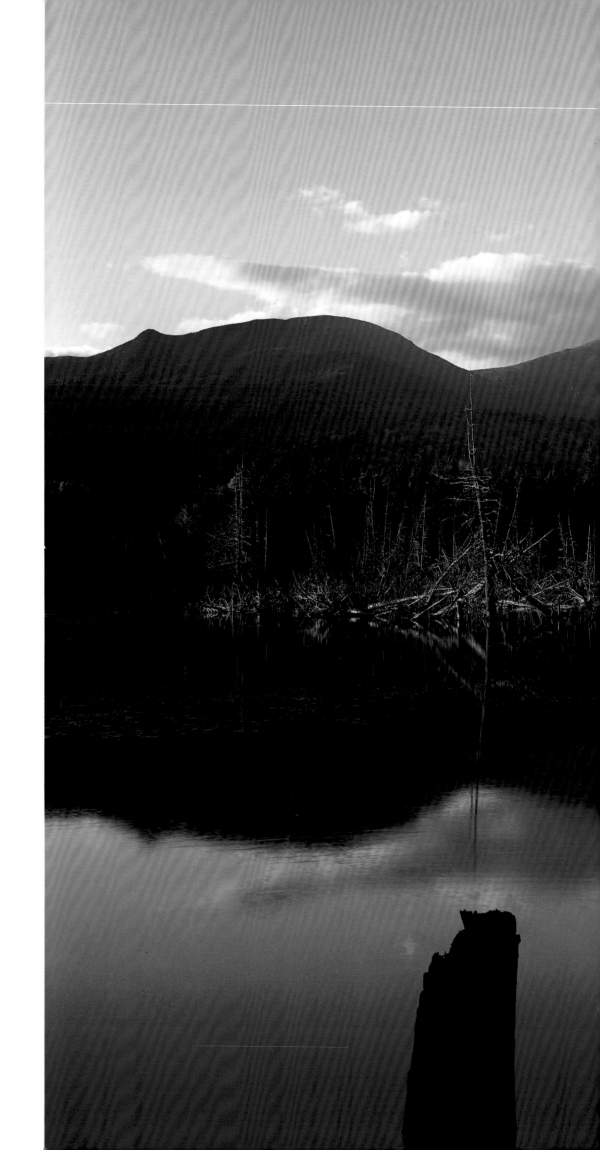

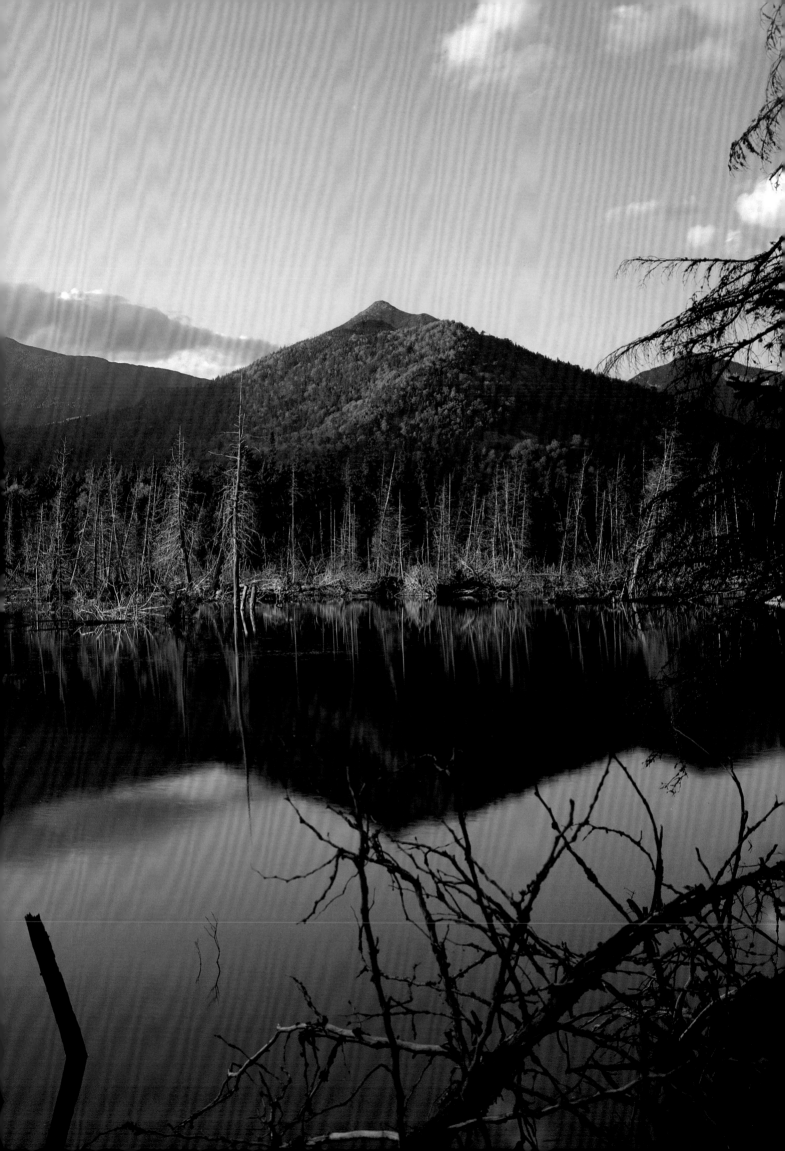

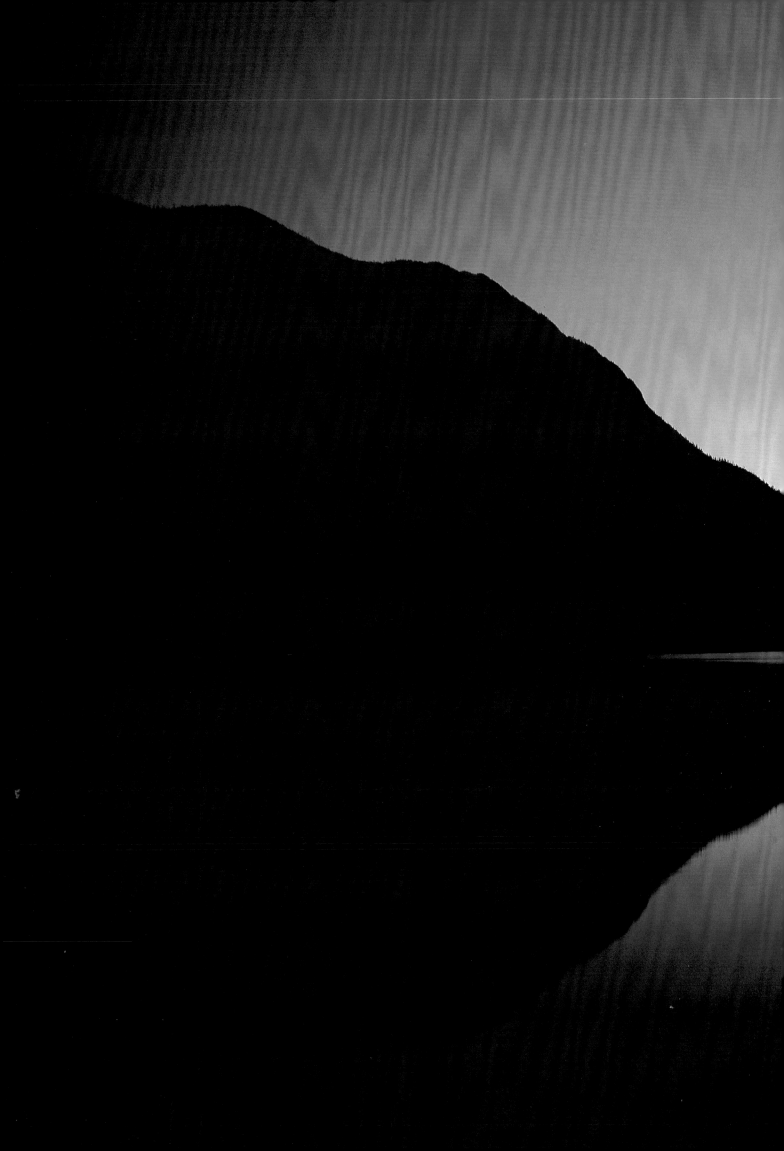

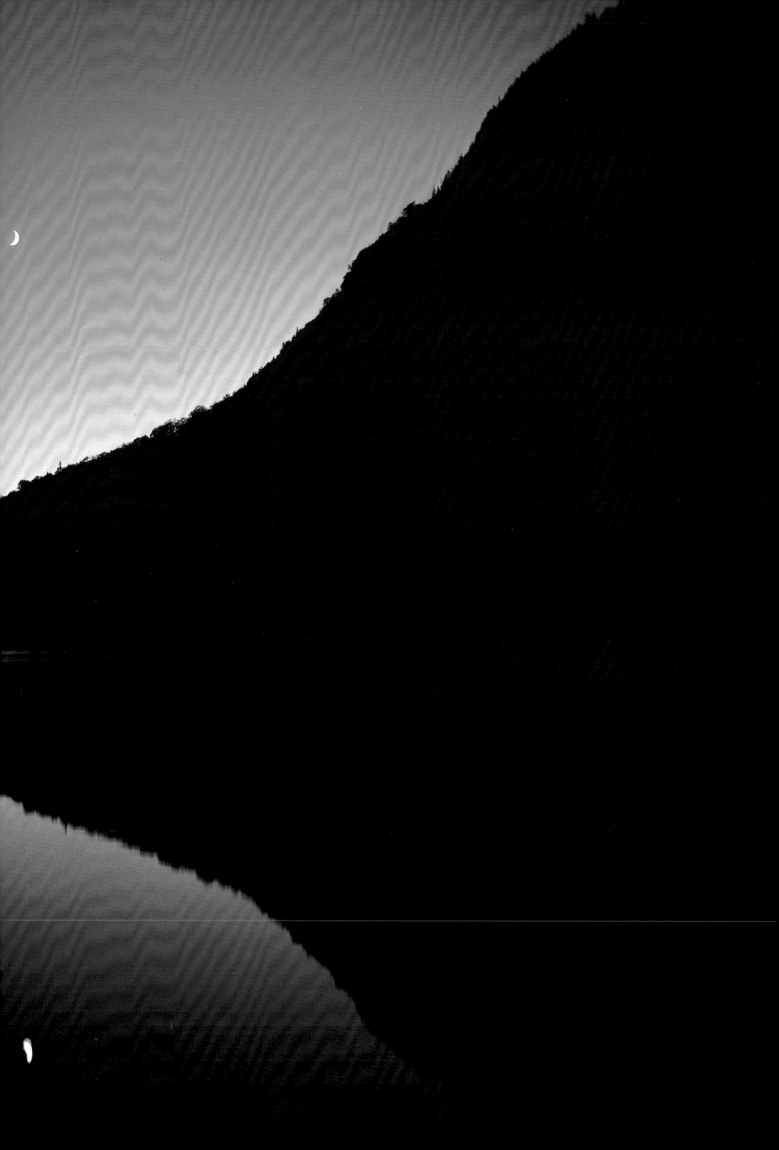

In the Woods

A French friend of mine commented, "Your photographs are so patriotic. You Americans love your woods so!" It is no doubt true. In some uniquely American way our woods and wilderness are our connection with the past, and consequently they also tell us something about our future. Europeans and Asians look to their ancient treasures of art and architecture for their heritage. As a young nation we lack a comparable tradition of civilization, but we have our virgin forests and primeval wildernesses, which span the ages to an even deeper and more distant past.

As a man tramps the woods to the lake, he knows he will find pines and lilies, blue heron and golden shiners, shadows on the rocks and the glint of light on the wavelets, just as they were in the summer of 1354, as they will be in 2054 and beyond. He can stand on a rock by the shore and be in a past he could not have known, in a future he will never see. He can be part of time that was and time yet to come.

William Chapman White in *Adirondack Country*

Pages 124–125: White birch

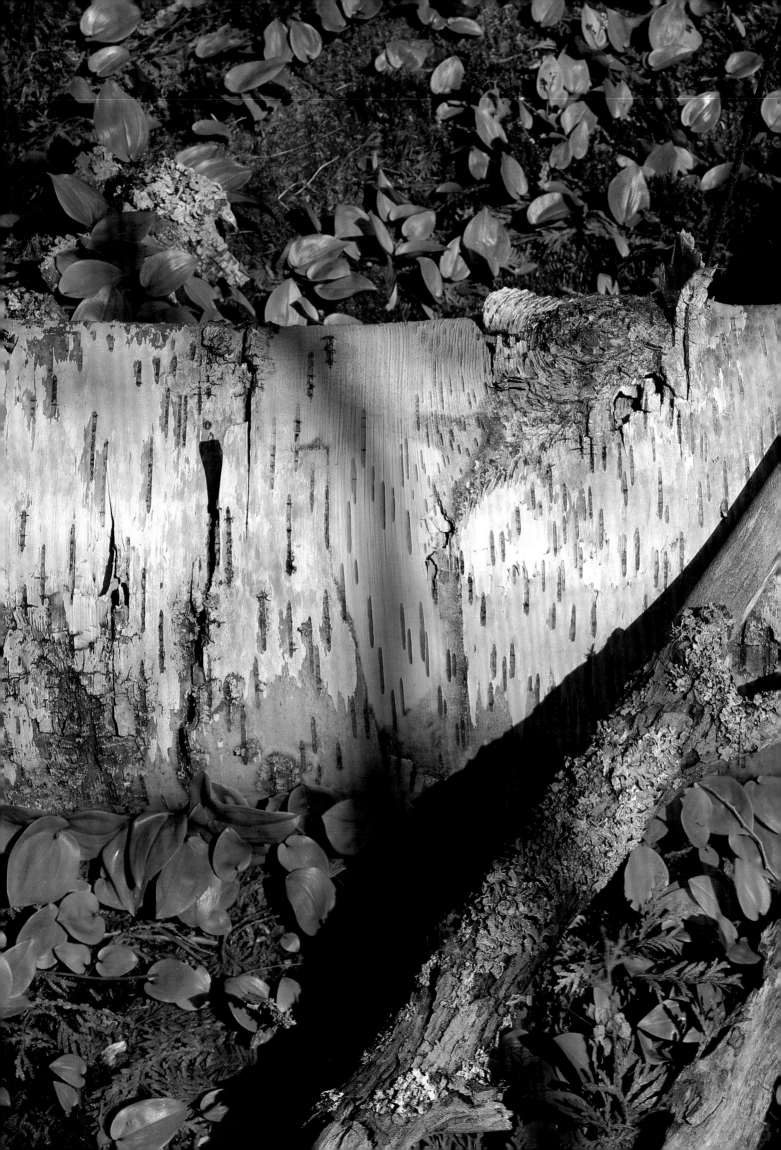

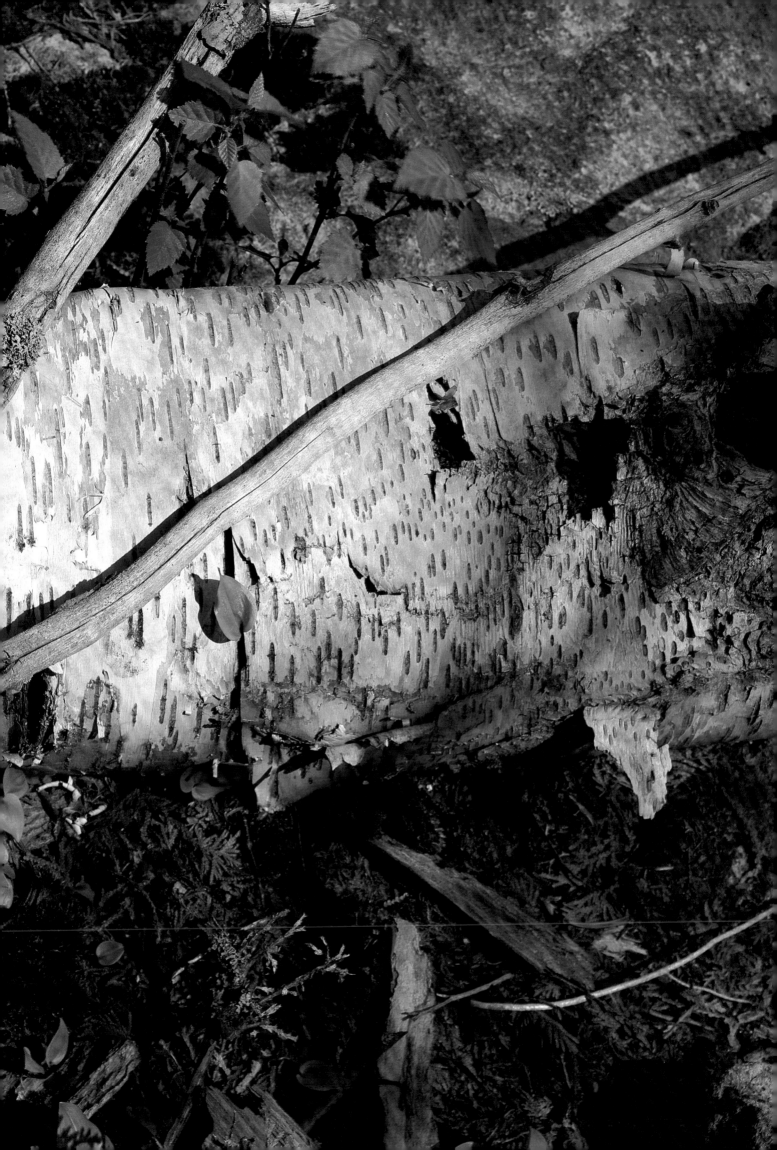

Near my childhood home in Lake Placid was a small wood, perhaps only four hundred yards from one end to the other, but it seemed large to a little boy. There were some very tall trees, a big rock outcropping, a sunny clearing, a marshy place with thick bushes, a stream that ran dry in the summer, and many trails. I went to play in my "forest" nearly every day. In those days we thought less about protecting nature, and trash was often left behind. In the last thirty years the woods have become much cleaner. The Adirondack Mountain Club, whose volunteer members have carried out tons of trash, deserve much credit. Their labors are part of a greater national awareness that our natural resources are limited. There is a new spirit that says, "Let's take care of this, perhaps the finest part of our heritage."

Page 127: Dusting of the first snow on Phelps Mountain

Pages 128–129: Birch trees in snow

Pages 130–131: Spring near Crystal brook

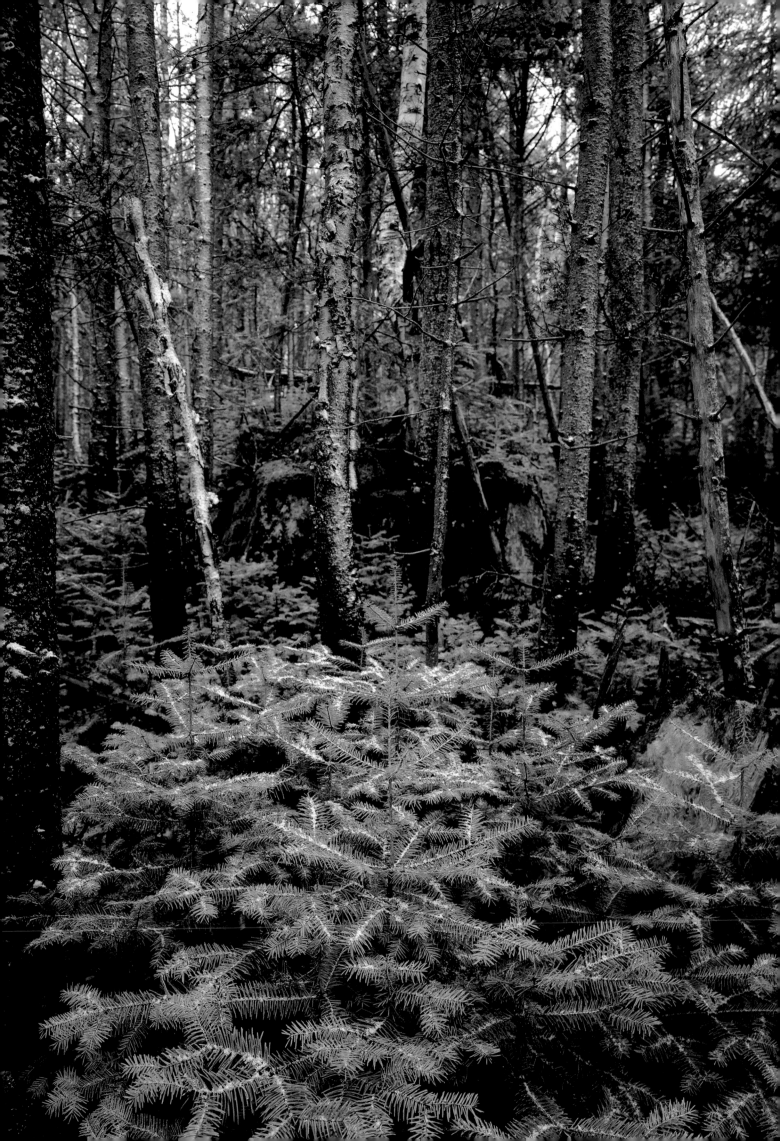

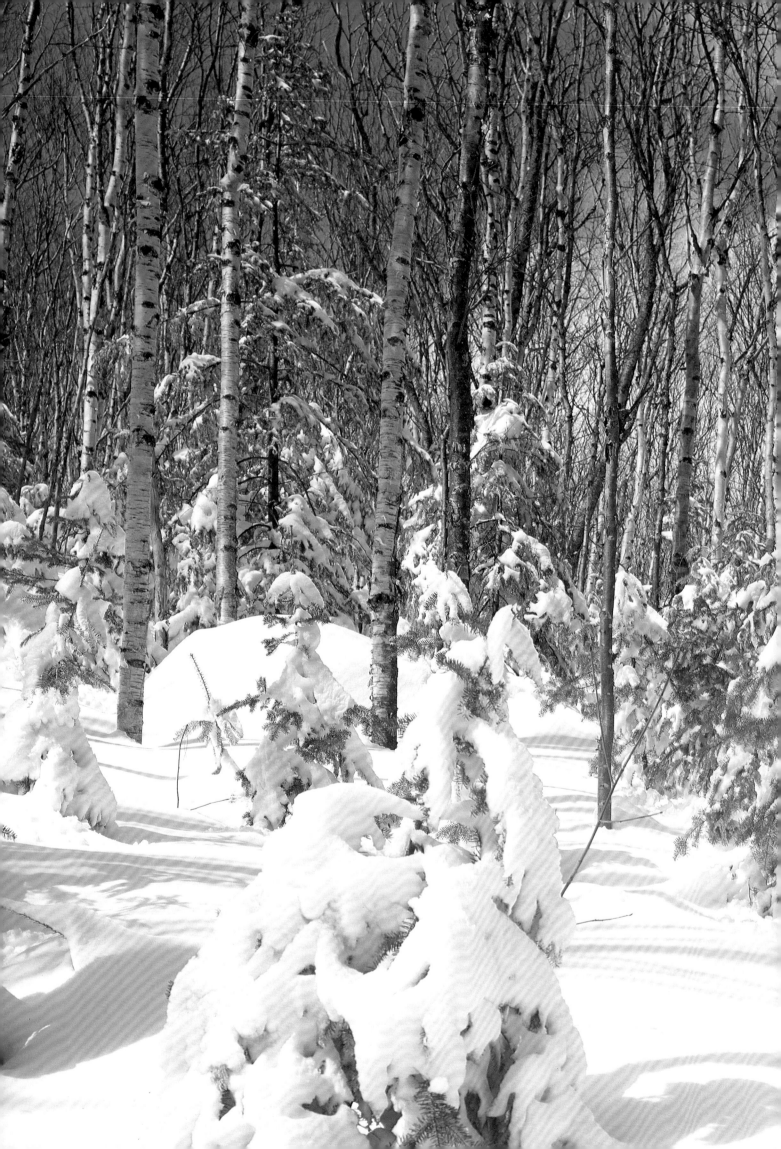

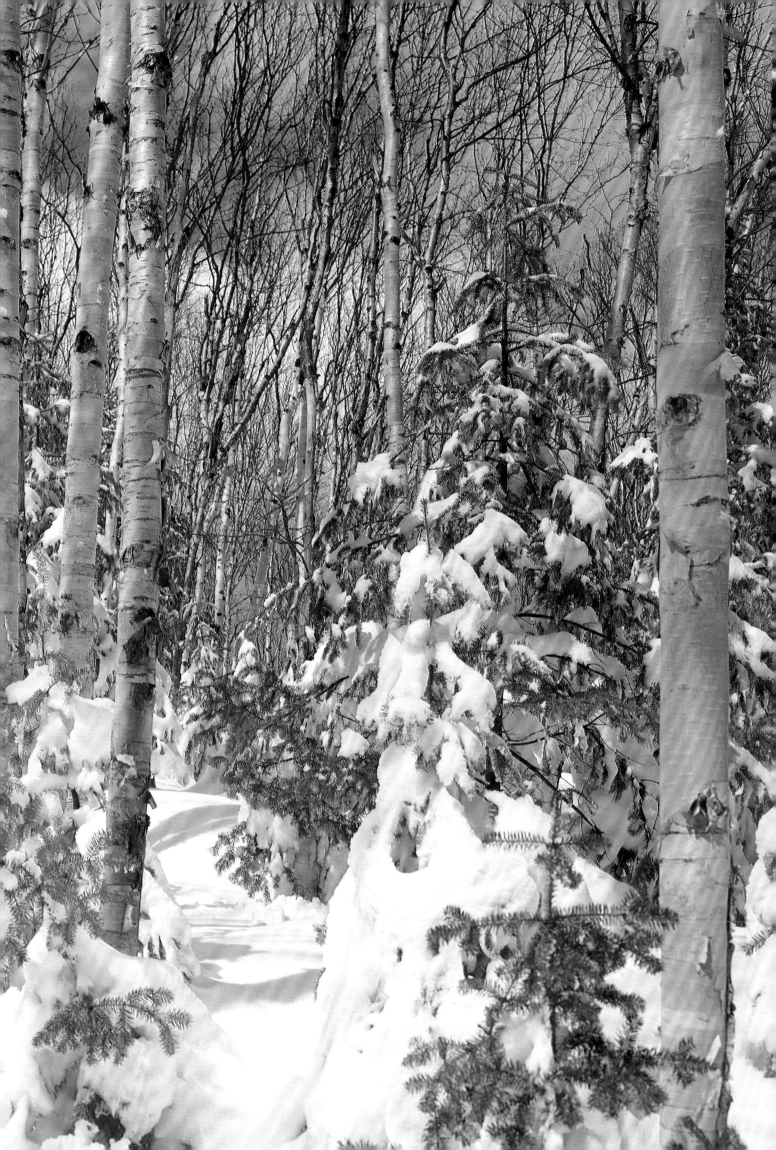

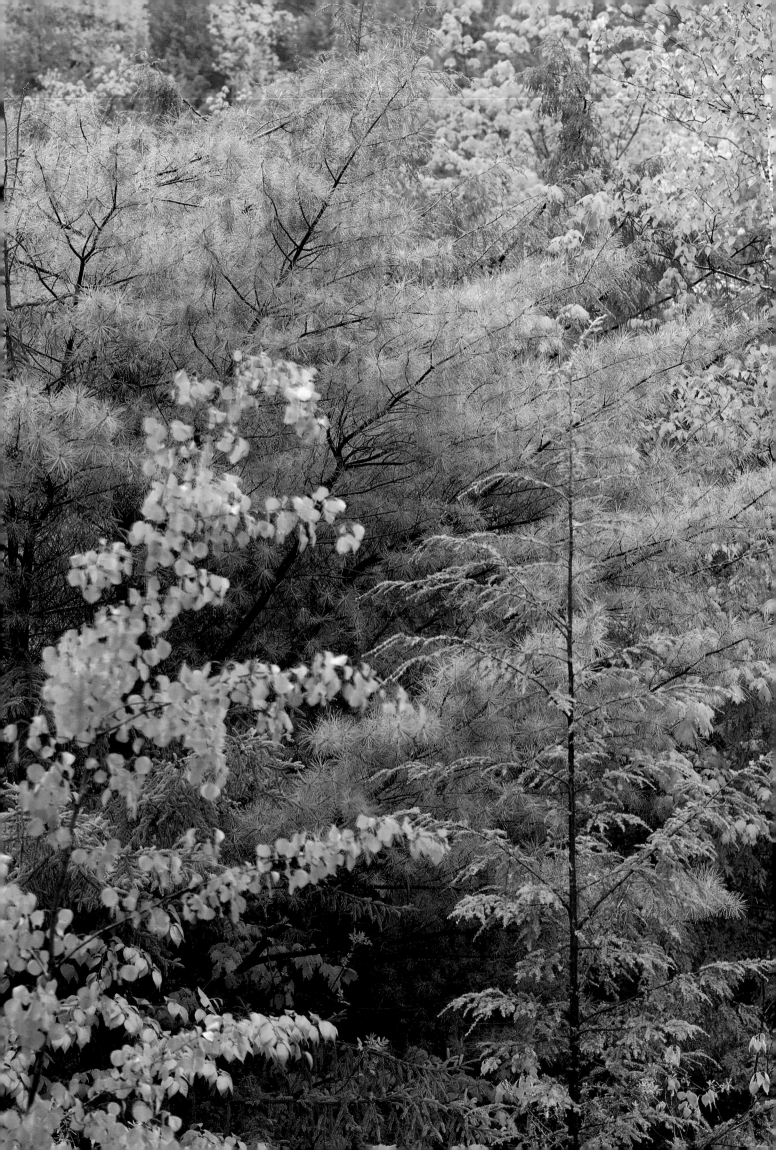

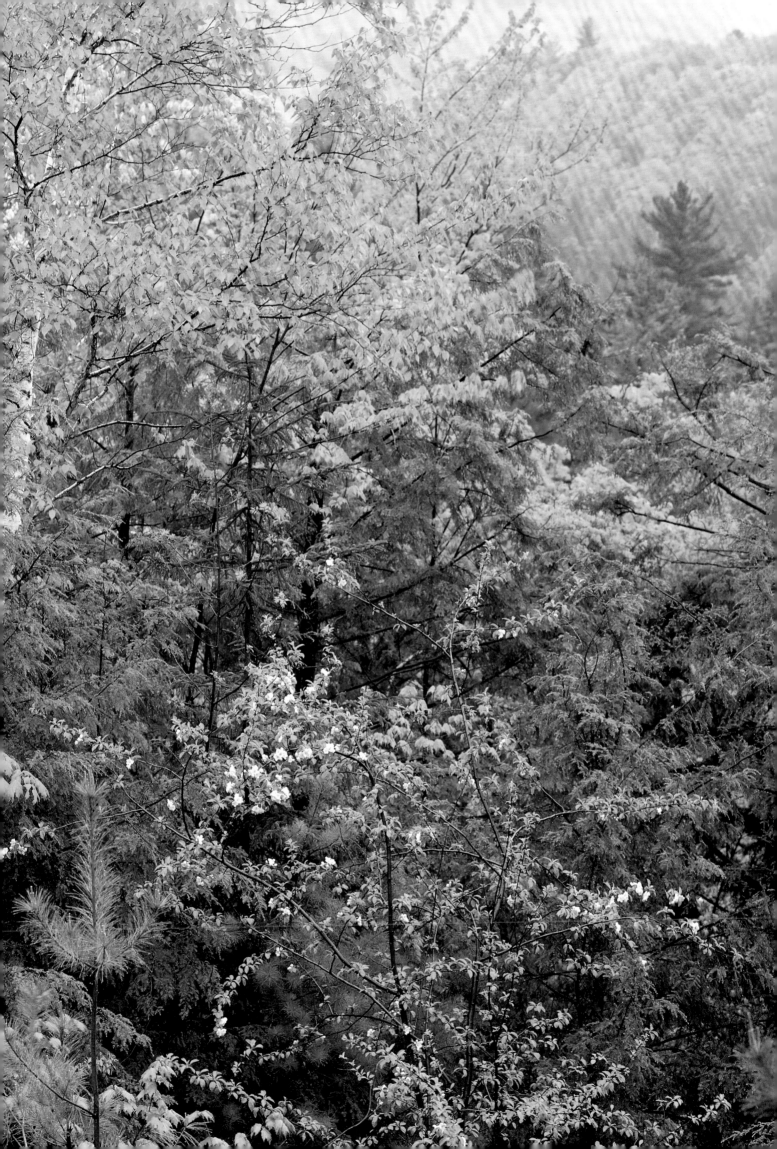

By the Road

To visit some of the scenes of the previous photographs one must walk half a mile from the road, to reach others, as far as twenty. The next sixteen photographs are taken close to the road and prove that there are also wonderful vistas to be seen along the highways.

Interstate 87, the Adirondack Northway, has been called America's most scenic highway. It runs along Schroon Lake and Schroon River for many miles on its way north to the Canadian border. Driving along the Northway one morning I became fascinated by the glimmer of Schroon River in the distance. I turned off at the next exit and backtracked on local roads until I came to a spot that was right for the photograph on page 175.

New York State Route 73 from the Northway to Lake Placid runs along Chapel Pond and the Upper and Lower Cascade lakes. The steep rock walls that rise out of these waters and define the trajectory of the highway are quite spectacular. There are roadside rest areas near each lake, and if one stops and briefly closes his ears to the occasional car going by, one can enter a peaceful world of scenic beauty.

New York State Route 30 between Tupper Lake and Long Lake winds its way through wetlands. At times, one has the impression of floating instead of driving through the area. The Blue Ridge Road from North Hudson to Newcomb stays high and affords grand views of the high peaks to the north and south. It traverses one of the least used and most sparsely populated regions in the park.

Pages 150–151: Lower Cascade Lake

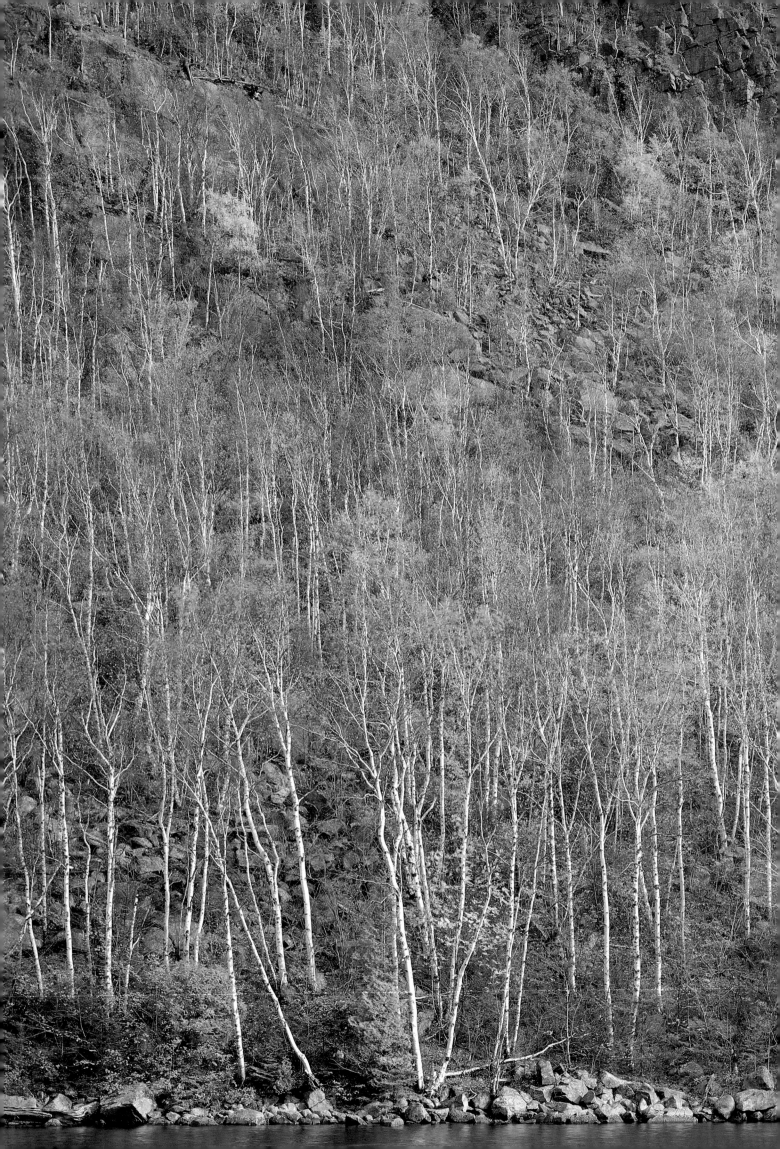

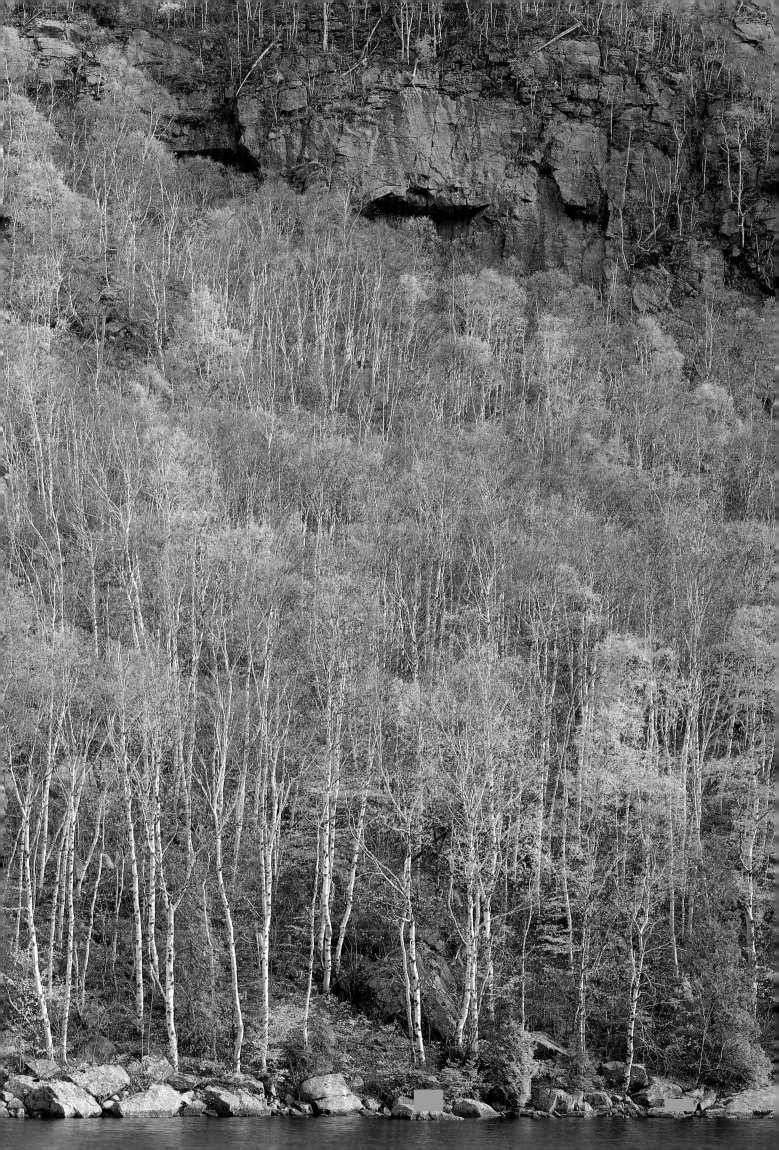

Sometimes roadside photography is more than a matter of convenience. I took the photograph on page 159 of Coreys Road, on a day when the temperature never rose above ten below zero Fahrenheit. Obviously winter photography poses its own special technical problems. Although Kodak warns there may be some loss of film speed under sub-zero conditions, I have never experienced this. However, batteries do freeze. I use two batteries in my equipment. One is in the Minolta Spotmeter, the other in the electronic shutter with which my 300 mm Schneider Symmar is outfitted. When both stopped working below the freezing point, I took them out of the equipment and kept them in a T-shirt pocket next to my body until I was ready to make the picture. Working this way, I was able to get only about three or four minutes' use before another ten-minute warm-up was necessary. I have also had problems with the bellows of the camera. When I first went out with my Deardorff and its new naugahide bellows in the frigid weather, I found that the naugahide froze and I could not close the camera. The manufacturer made a special set of pigskin bellows and asked me to field-test them. I was happy to report to Jack Deardorff that they were perfect.

The queen of the mountain roads is the Whiteface Memorial Highway, which winds its way up toward the top of this 4867 foot peak. Built as a WPA project and dedicated by Franklin Delano Roosevelt in 1935 to the veterans of World War I, it is a toll road open to tourists from mid-spring to mid-fall. The last photograph in this book was taken from this road late one September afternoon. The mountain top was shrouded in clouds. I set up my camera at about four thousand feet, just below the mist, and faced the dramatic sunset.

Page 153: Ausable Chasm

Pages 154–155: The Nubble at Giant Mountain

Pages 156–157: Round Mountain at Chapel Pond

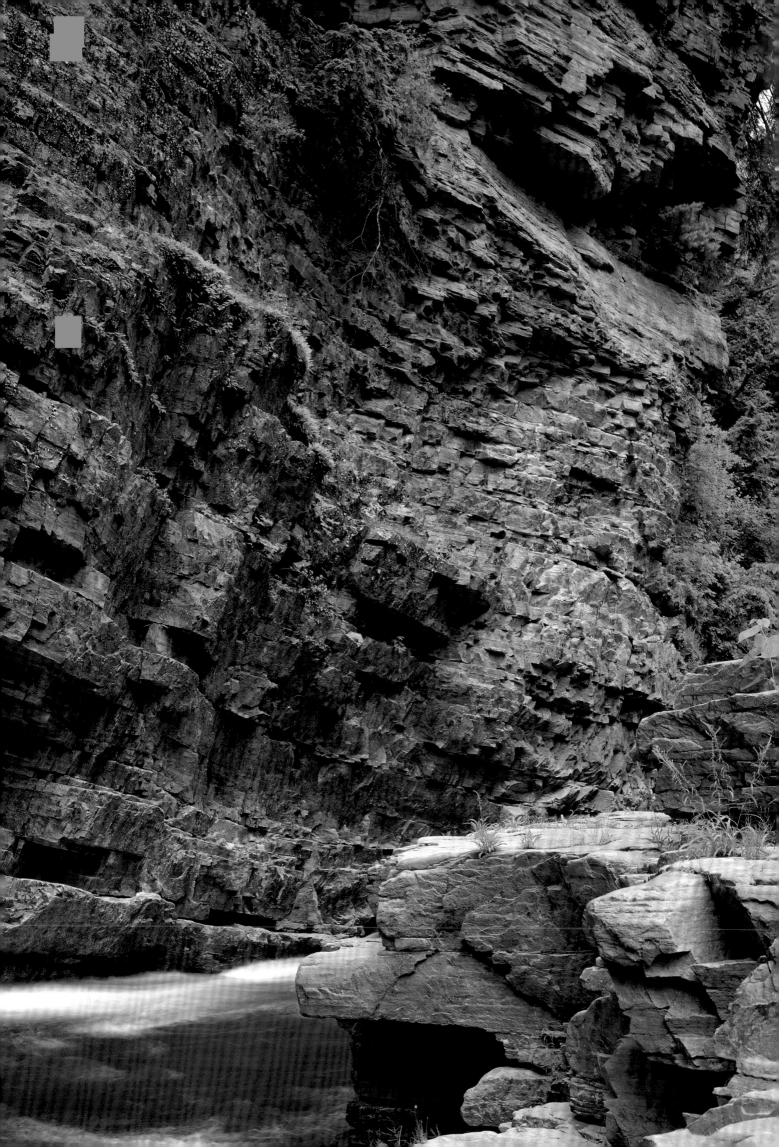

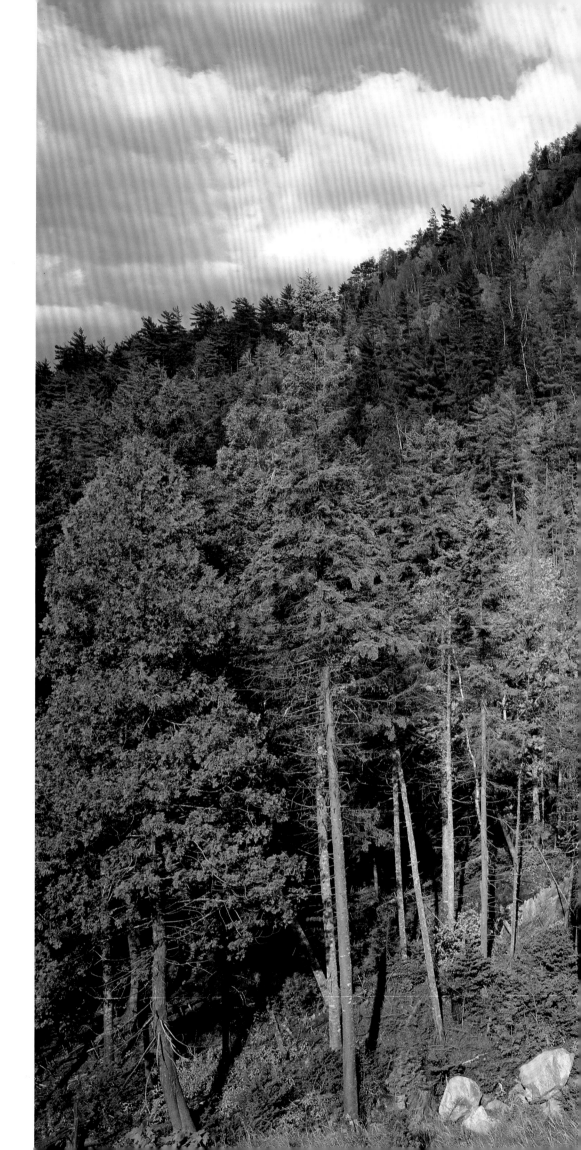

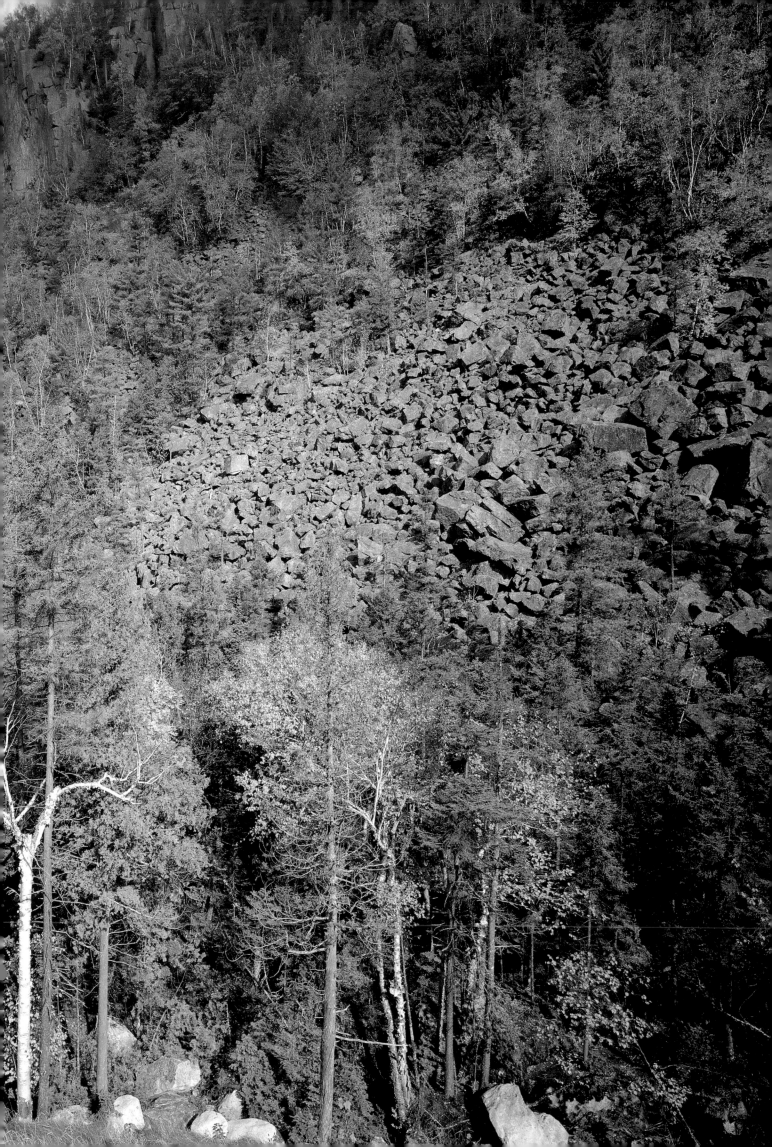

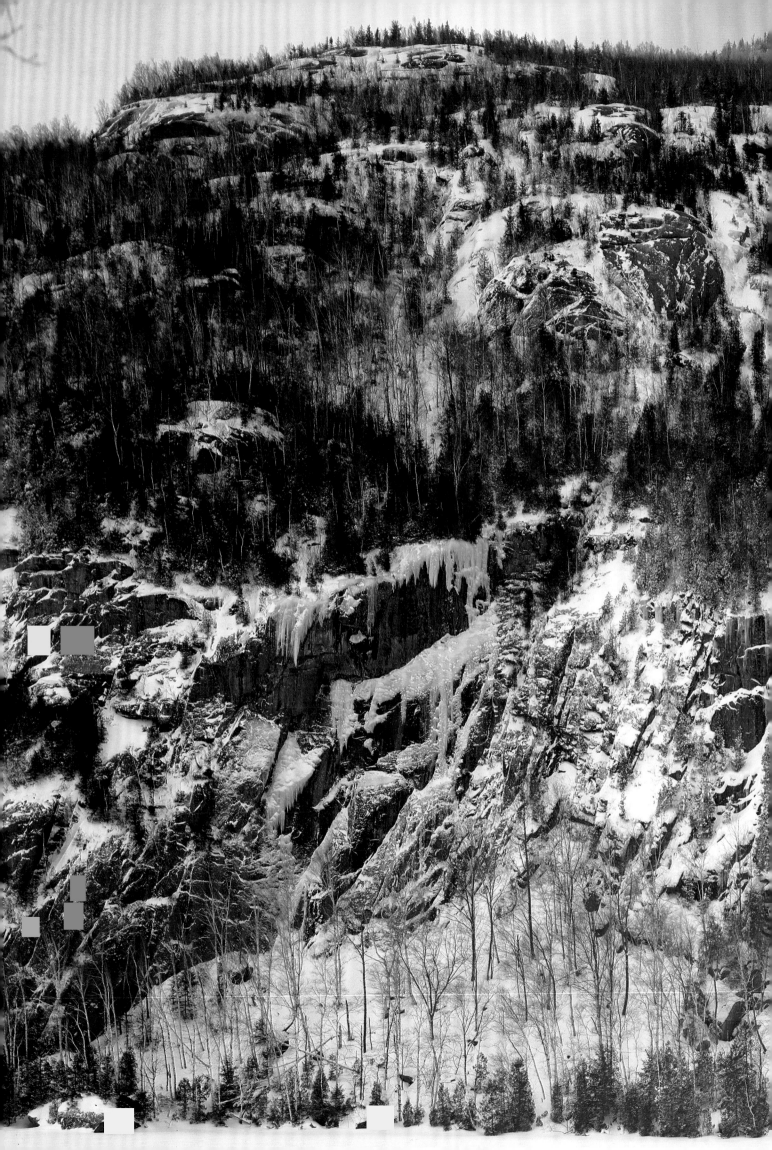

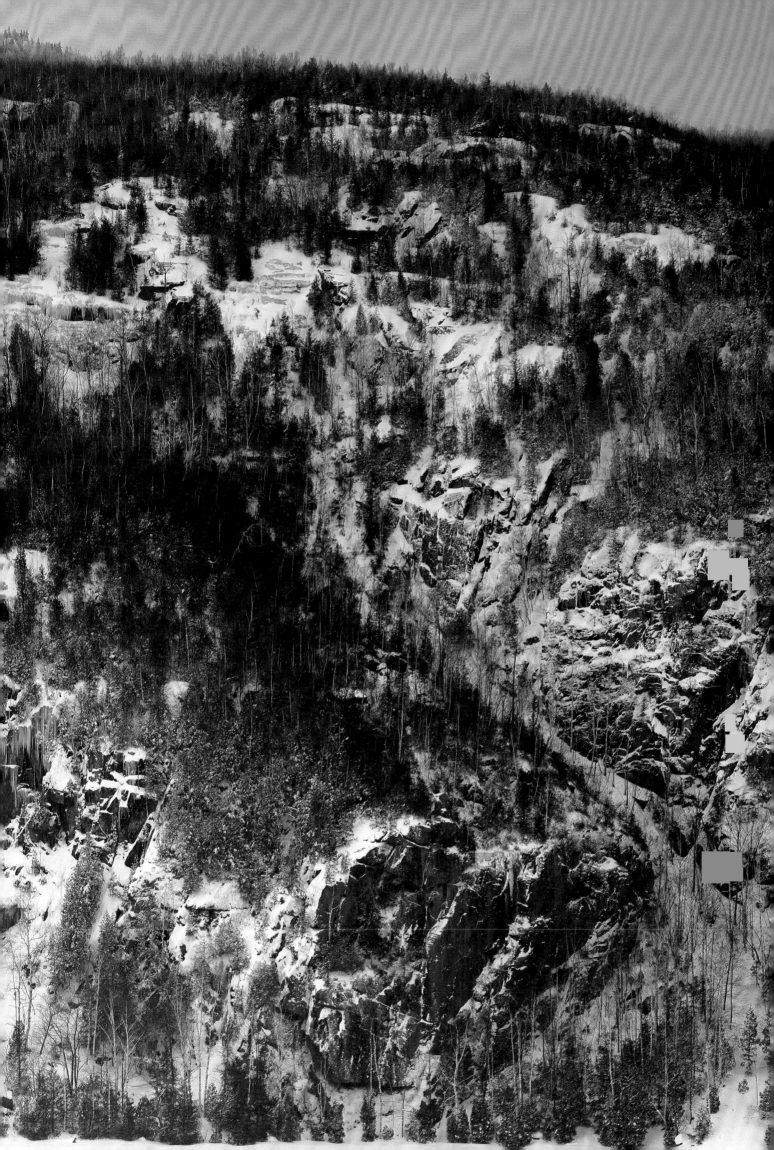

Page 159: Coreys Road near Saranac Lake

Pages 160–161: River Road near Lake Placid

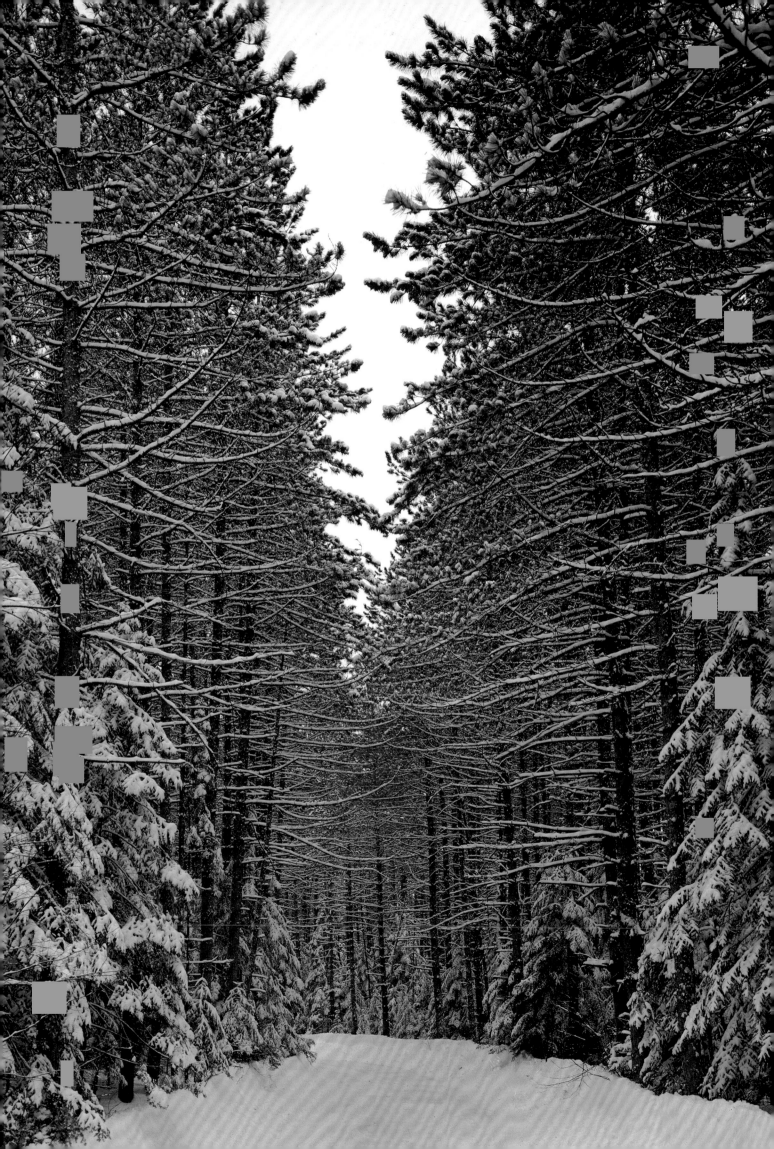

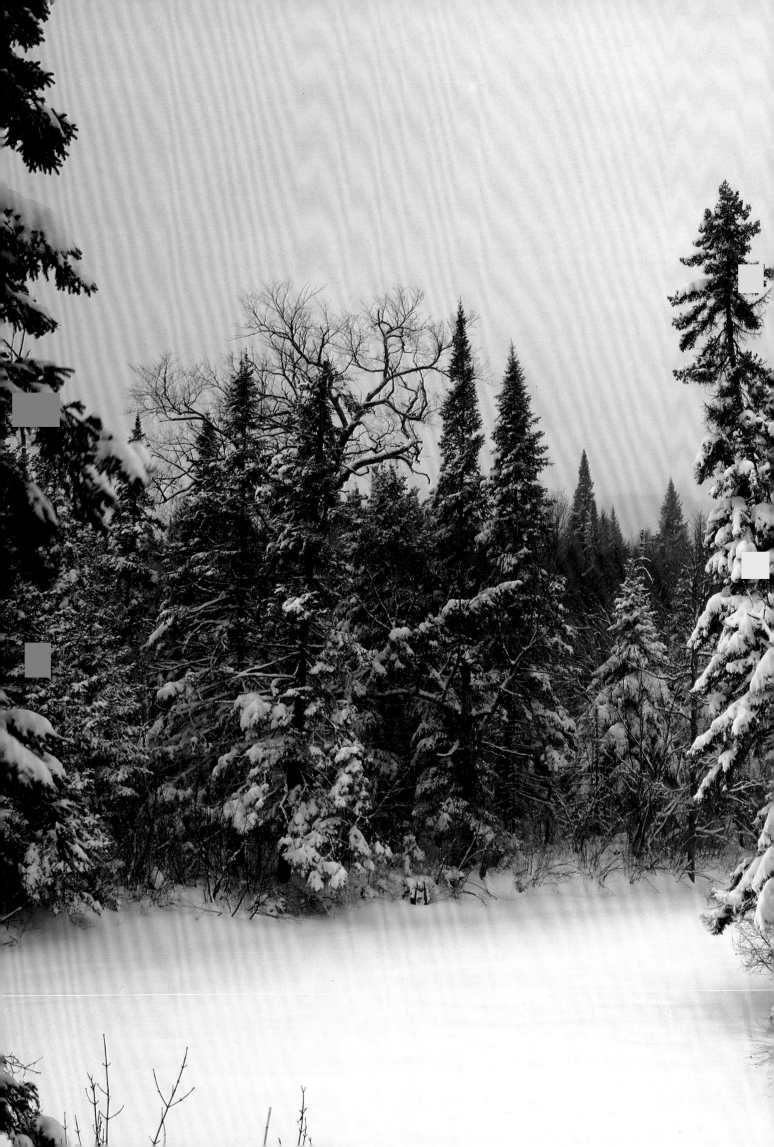

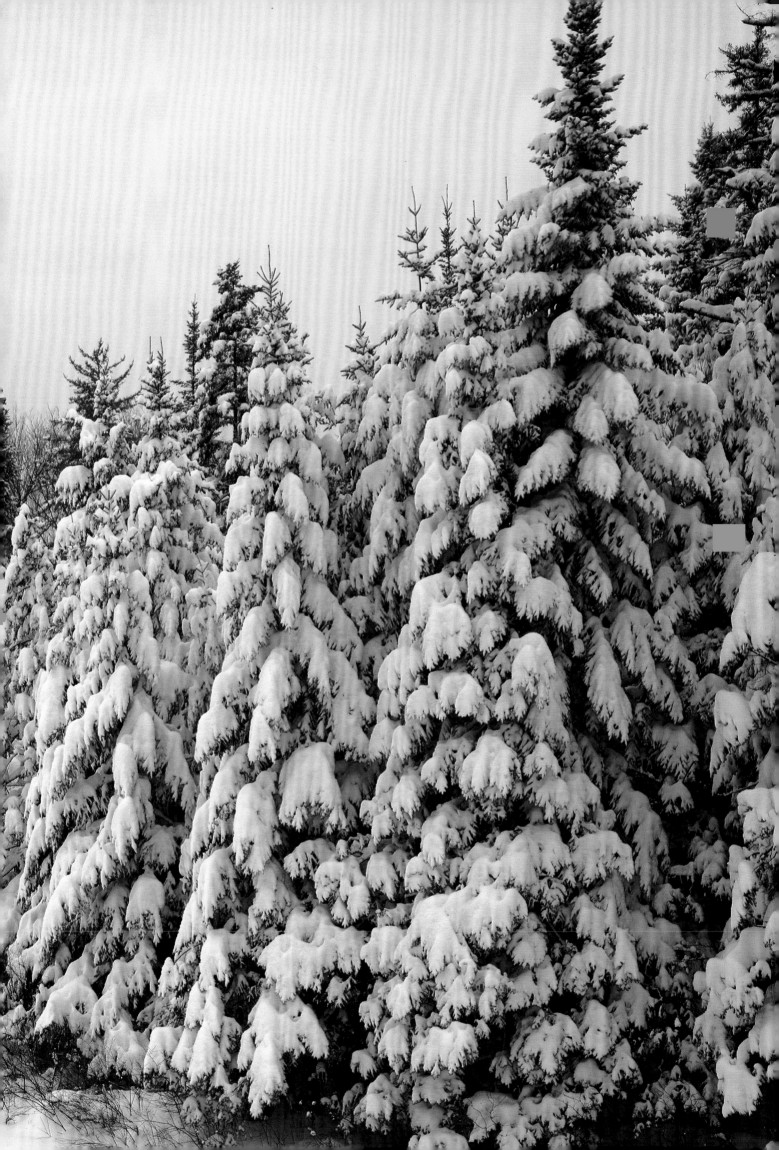

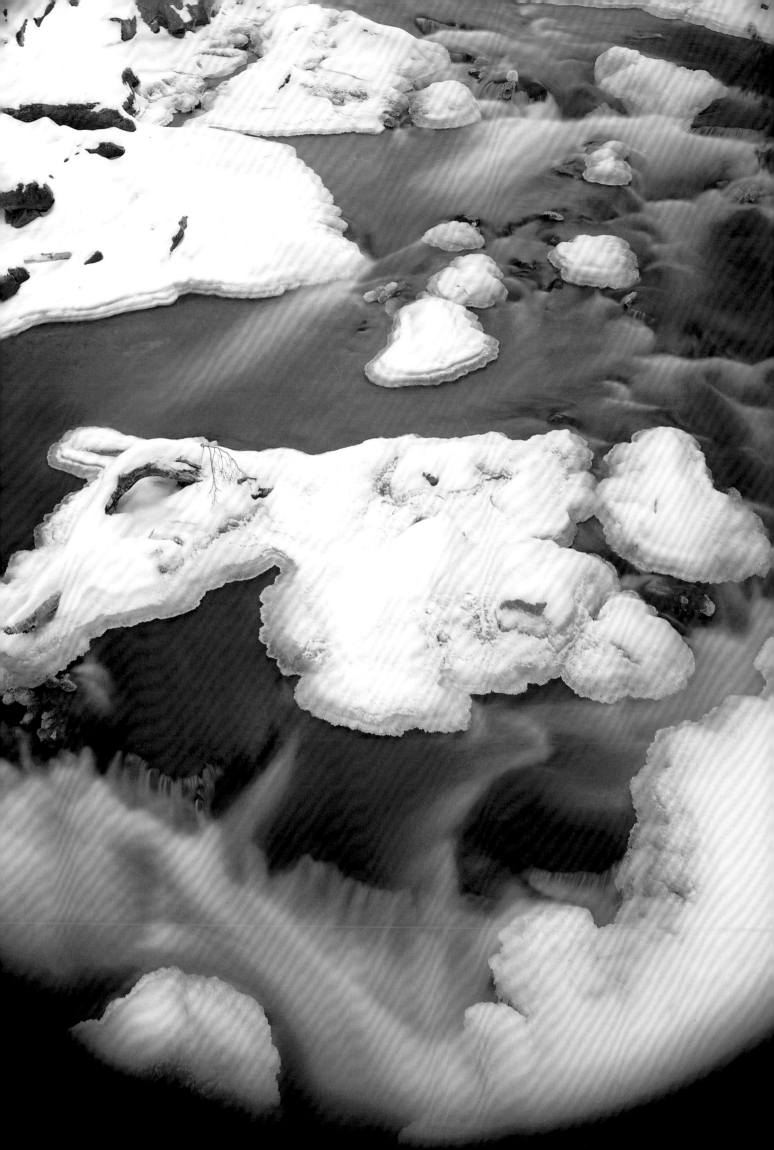

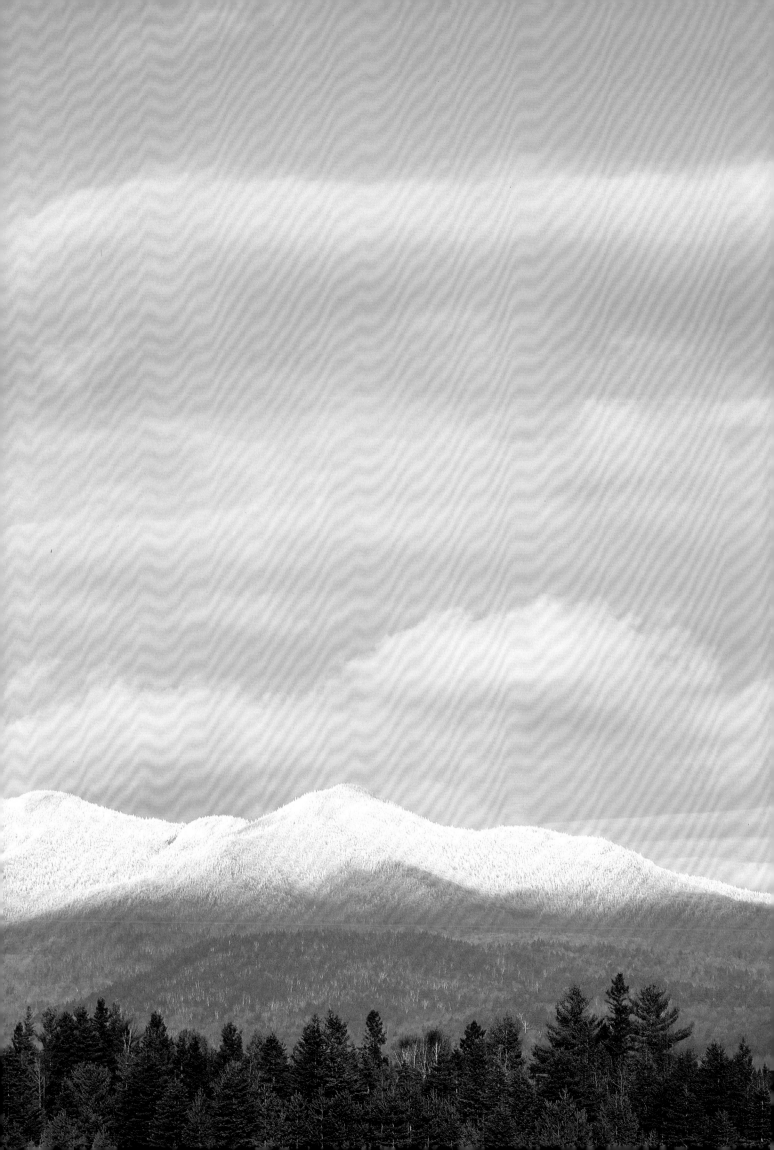

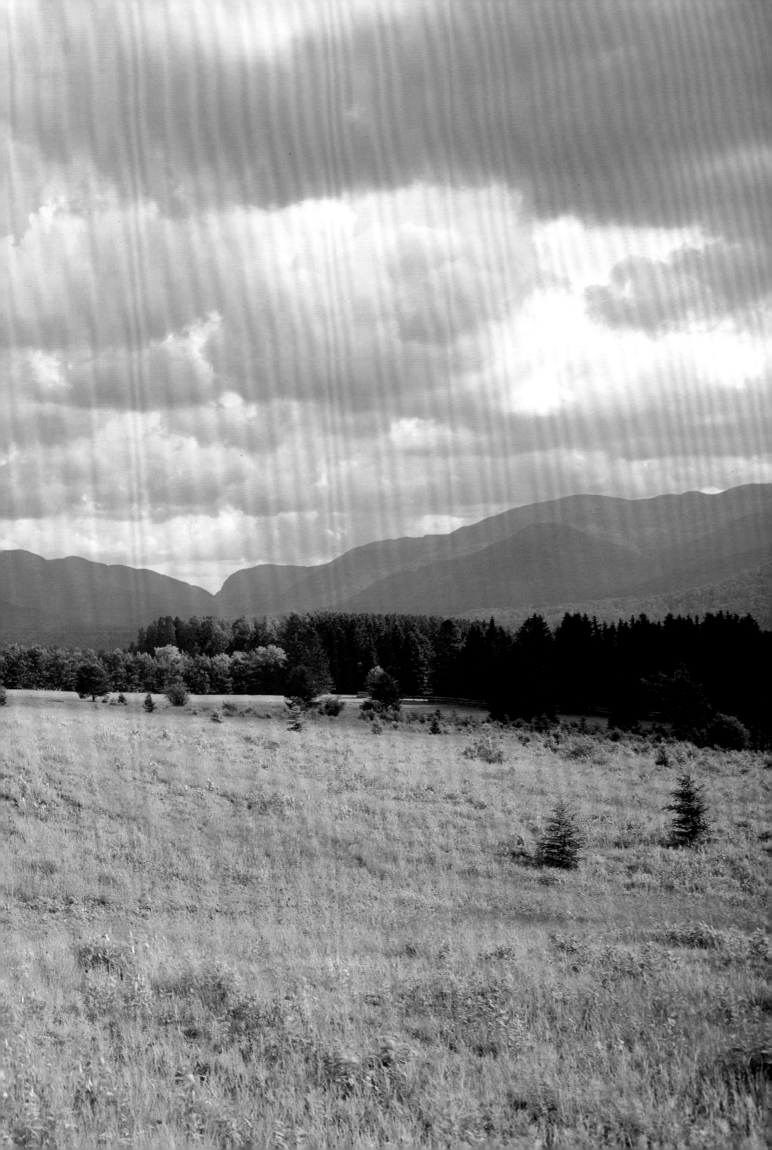

Page 169: High Falls Gorge

Pages 170–171: Lake Placid

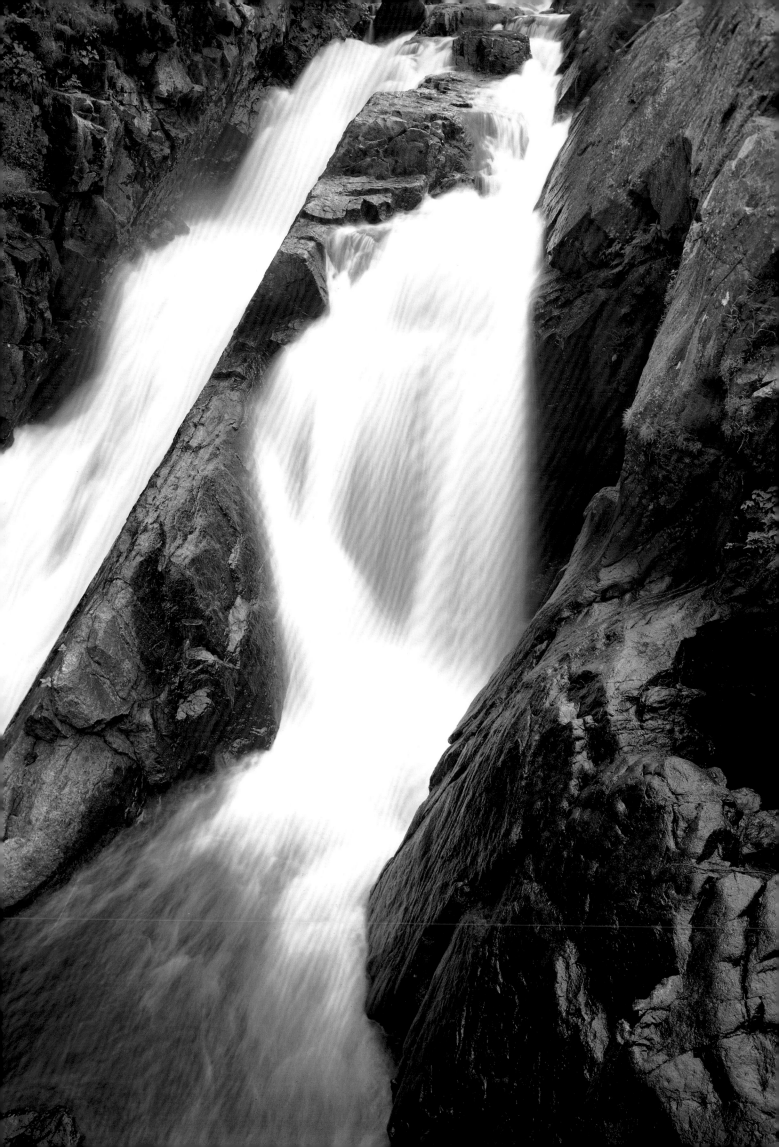

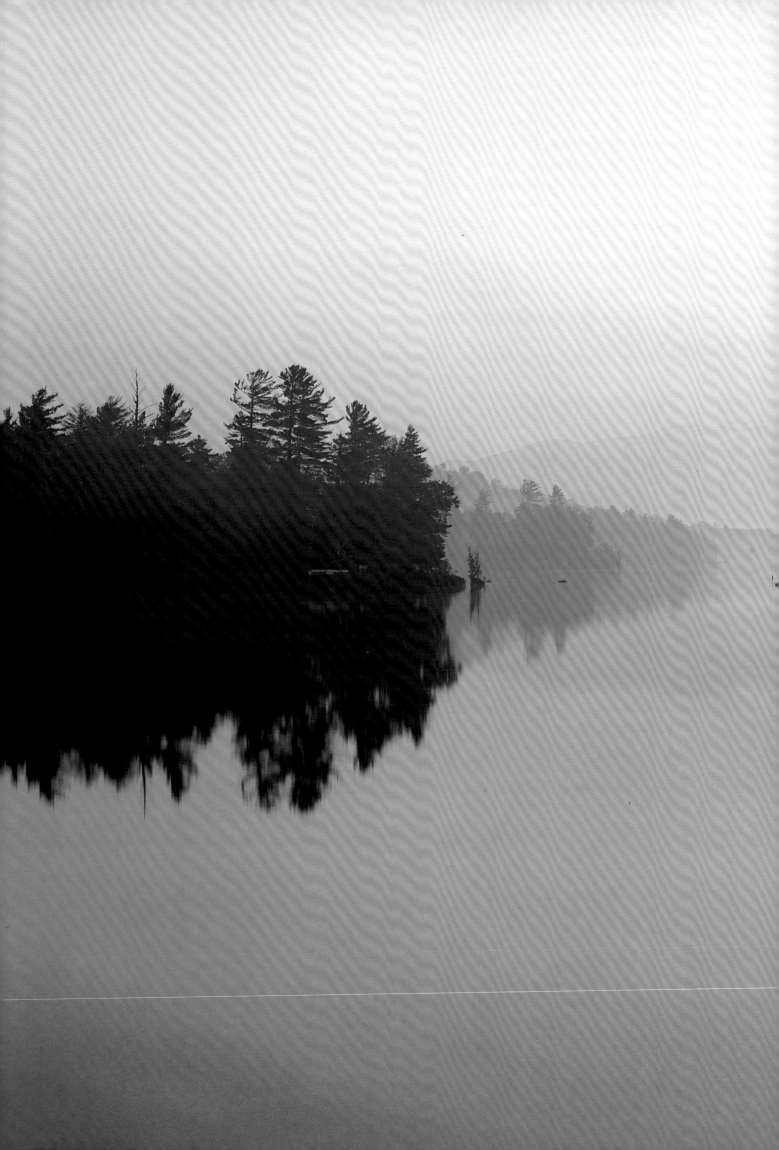

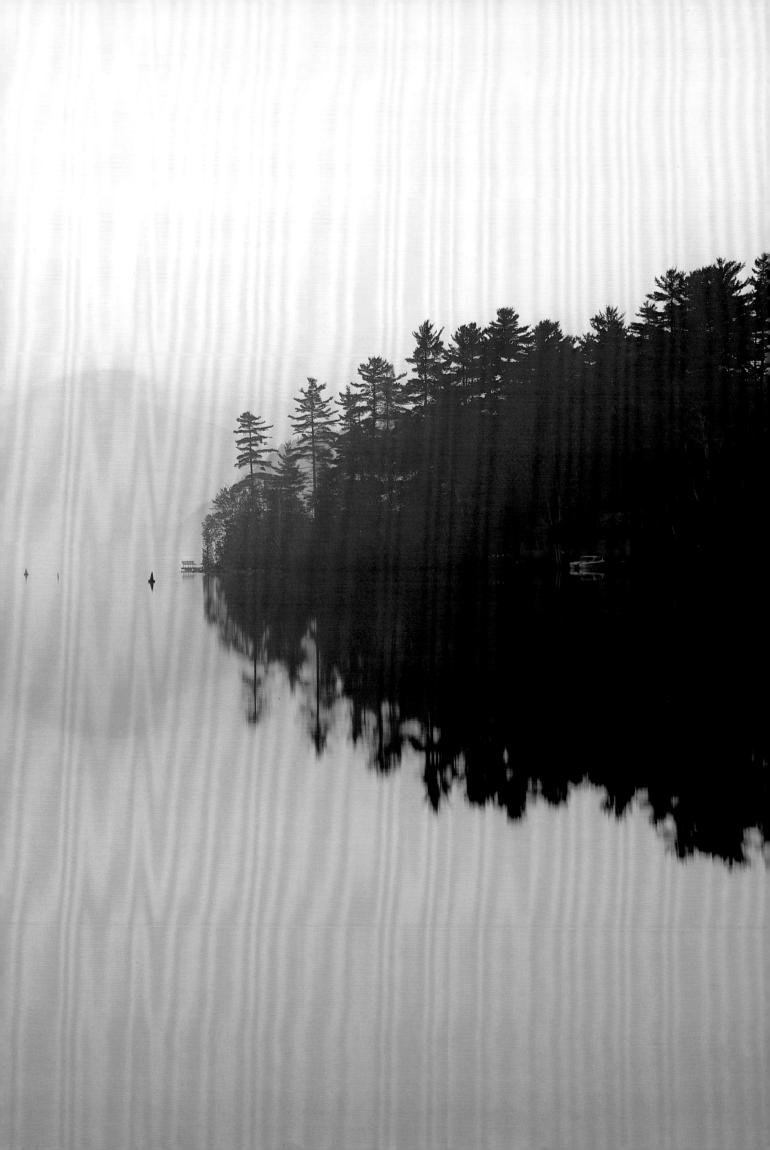

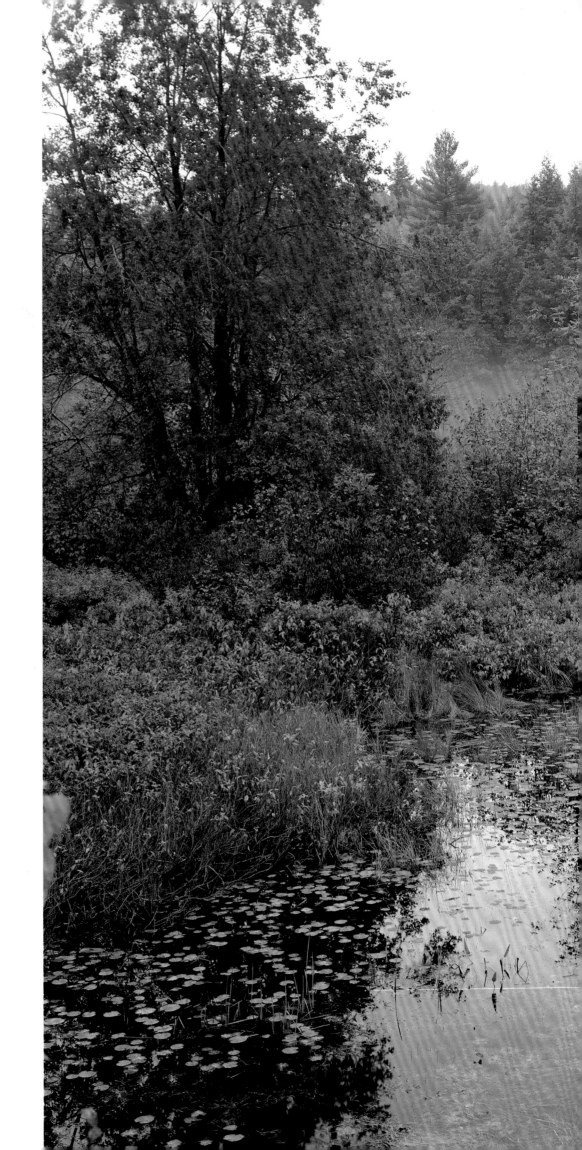

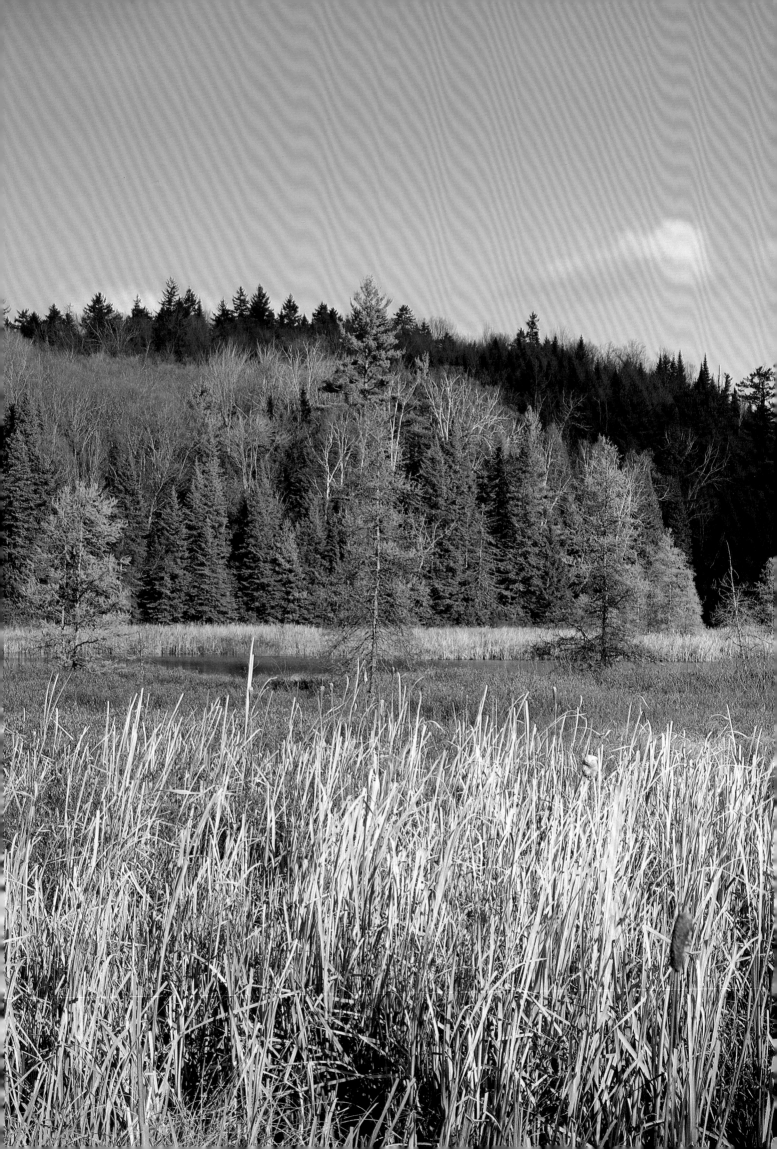

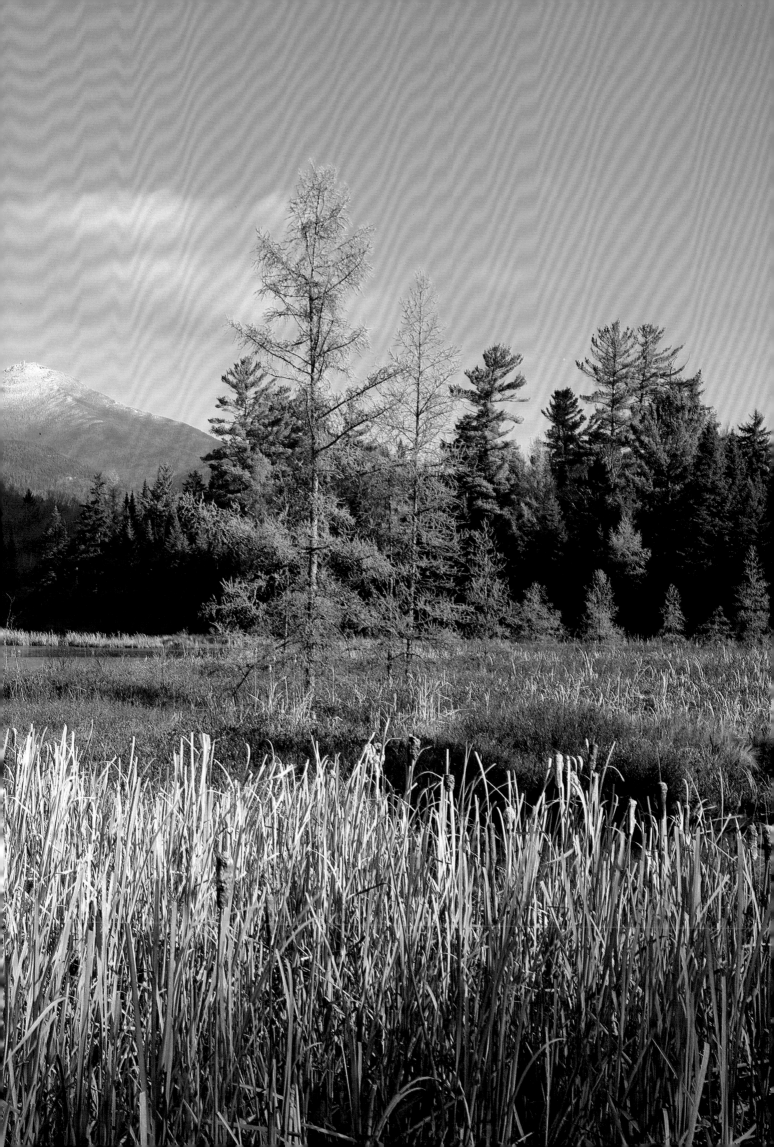

Page 179: Chapel Pond

Pages 180–181: Sunset over Lake Placid and the McKenzie Range from Whiteface Mountain

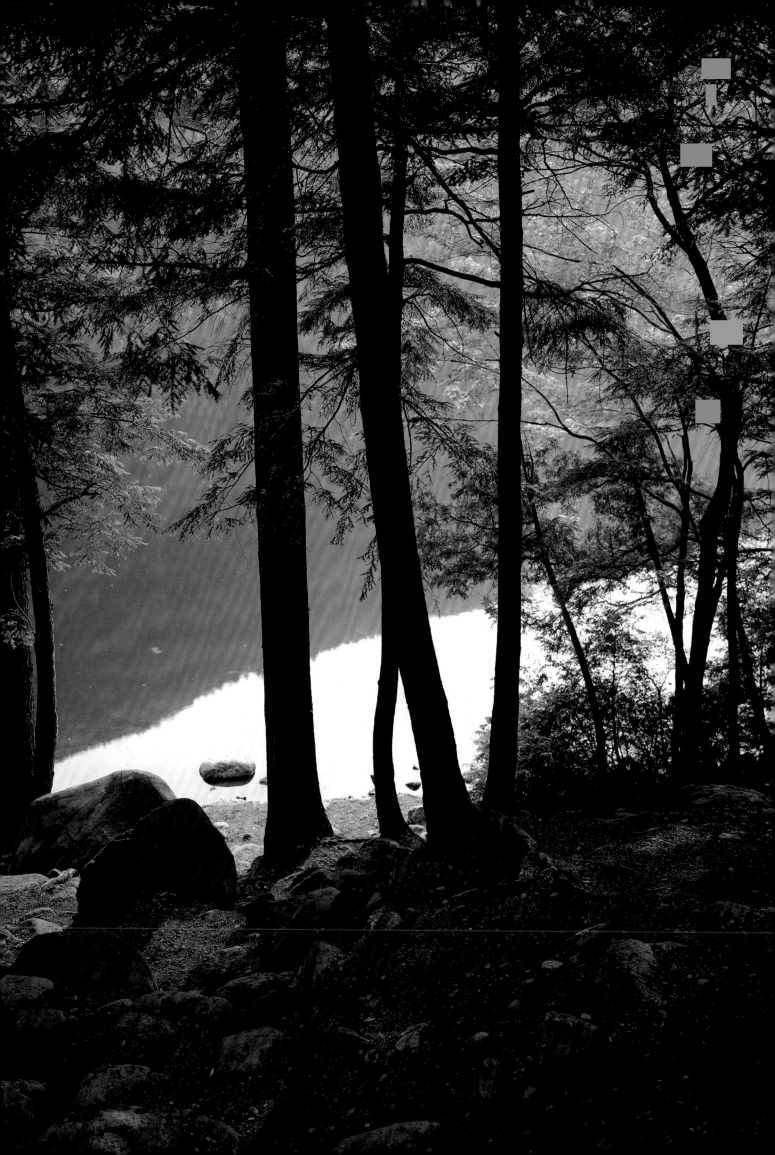

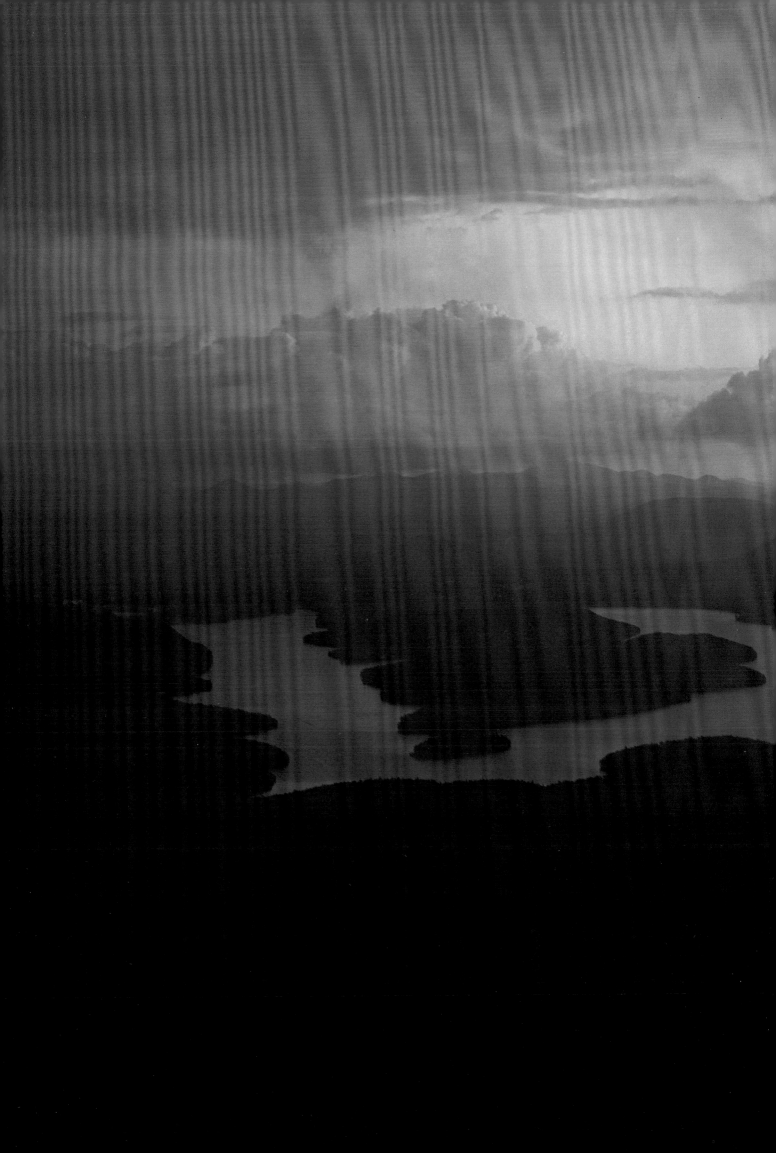

The Adirondack Park

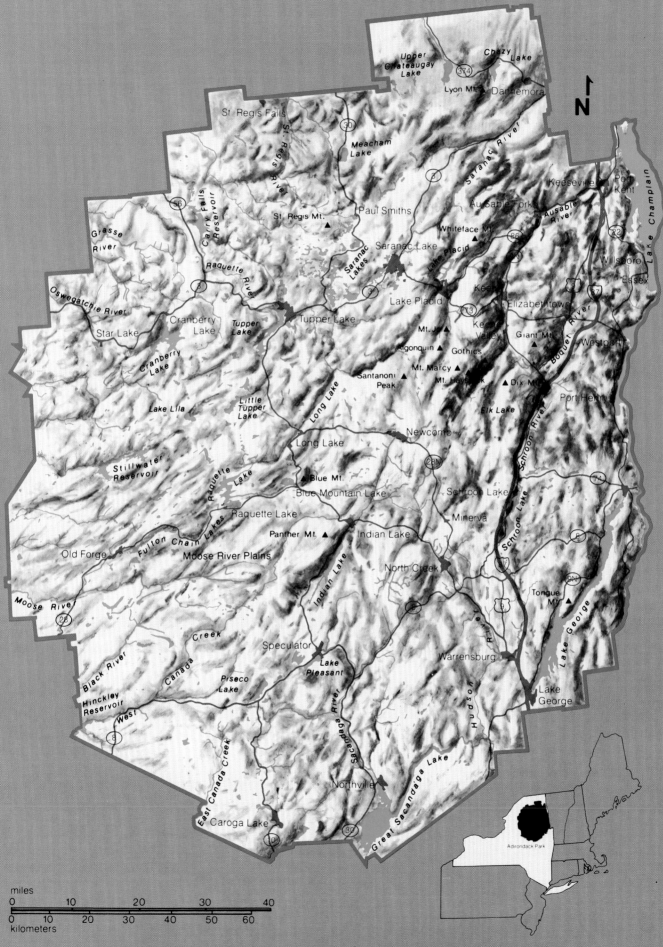

Northeast United States

miles
0   10   20   30   40
0 10 20 30 40 50 60
kilometers

© 1985 Anne E. Lacy

183